John, Jesus, & Me

Jeremy Vance

GRACE THEOLOGY PRESS

CONTENTS

Foreword v

Preface 1

Introduction 3

1. The Gift of Eternity 5

2. Drink the Water 13

3. Eat the Bread 21

4. Why Me? 33

5. Who is Your Shepherd? 43

6. "Recombobulation" 53

7. Open to Love 65

8. I Have Decided to Follow Jesus 75

9. The Work of the Holy Spirit 85

10. Love At Its Utmost 95

11. God So Loves . . . Now Love 105

FOREWORD

Each generation has the responsibility to reach and influence those around them. It's something that all who claim Christ as Savior know to be true. John the Baptist was the first to point to Jesus as the One who came to save the world by giving His life for many. His life and message changed the world as we know it. And still does. That message is the love of our heavenly Father. As a person who works with many people on a day to day basis, both believers and non-believers, I'm often asked about the evidences of faith. I point, almost always, to the millions of changed lives who found the love that only the Father gives.

Jesus' life gave us a pattern of obedience and love. It's a pattern that we can follow today, and the gospel of John is a great place to find it. From the beginning to the end, it's made clear that there is lots of work to be done. All of us are called to work within our own vocation and lifestyle to make an impact for the Kingdom. From formal ministry to the market place, we are commissioned to use this message of love, and go out and make disciples.

Regrettably, not very many believers seem to understand all that this entails, at least when it comes to the importance in our daily living. Even people in leadership positions struggle with the idea of teaching others to see and experience God's love. Many people struggle accepting the love of the Father. They don't fully grasp one of the crucial pieces of the gospel message, which is love.

This is why this book, *John, Jesus, & Me,* is such a privilege for me to share—it helps us copy how Jesus shared the Father's love. It keeps it simple and in the Word of God. When I first started leading Bible Studies, one of my mentors challenged me never to stray away from Scripture. It was the best advice I was ever given, not only for my own life, but also for those in my sphere of influence. The truth of Scripture is what changes lives. We just need to point people to it and help them understand it. The Word of God stands true through the course of time. And since God's love is at the center of it all, it makes sense that this topic has to be one of a disciple maker's first priority.

The strength and validity of this book, *John, Jesus, & Me,* comes right out of the person to person interactions Jeremy has had with people. Jeremy's own experience of sharing God's love with many is what makes this book so real. Jeremy writes from many years of dedicated service of being a difference maker in the lives of others. For years he has been actively involved in shaping lives through the love of the Father. There are many people in his sphere of influence that would point to him as their example and mentor and teacher. His approach reflects a man who is rooted in Scripture and all that it brings.

—Perry Krosschell
Director of Missions and Vision
Pizza Ranch Inc.

PREFACE

I am not the most dynamic evangelist. Unlike some, when I talk to people, even though I want them to know the Lord loves them, I find the conversation does not go in that direction as often as I would like. However, when the conversation moves to talking about spiritual things, and they are open to knowing more about His love, I will say to them, "Read the Bible. Specifically, read the Gospel of John. Read it like a love letter written to you." Then I'll give some guidance, "When you read a love letter, you read it over and over. You read it slowly so you don't miss any of the meaning, because you really want to know how much the other person loves you."

Not too long ago, I realized it had been a long time since I had read the Gospel of John like God's love letter to me. So, I decided to open up my Bible and do what I had been telling others to do. When I did, I found that even though I have been a Christian for a long time, rereading the Gospel of John like God's love letter to me was so moving I felt I wanted to share how it made an impact on my heart and life.

When I say the Bible is "God's love letter" I feel I have to bring some clarity to what I mean by "God." God is one being, however, He exists in three persons—God the Father, God the Son (known as Jesus), and God the Holy Spirit. Throughout this book (and throughout the Bible as well as throughout the Gospel of John) these three persons, yet one God, are intermixed together. The love that

God has for each of us is seen in how His three persons all work to build this wonderful relationship with us.

My hope for this book—which takes eleven different moments from the Gospel of John and expands on them—is that it will help you see that God in His three persons really does love you. His love can have a profound effect on you and literally change your life. My hope and prayer is that the Lord will use this book to clarify the relationship He desires to have with each of us as we go deeper in knowing what it means that God so loves us!

—Jeremy Vance

INTRODUCTION

Have you ever been at a sporting event, or watched them on television where someone in the crowd is holding up a sign that reads, "John 3:16"? Most people know that person who got himself or herself in the eye of the camera is trying to tell the world about Jesus. That reference on their sign has become probably the most famous quote from Jesus. There are slight variations in our English translations of the Bible, yet here is that quote straight from the mouth of Jesus, "For this is how God loved the world: He gave his one and only Son, so that everyone who believes in him will not perish but have eternal life." There is a lot packed into that single verse.

Years ago I was at a Billy Graham crusade in Milwaukee, Wisconsin, and the Reverend Billy Graham preached on this very quote from Jesus. He said in his powerful Southern accent, "Where the word 'world' is in that verse, put your name in there. God so loved *you* that He gave His one and only Son." Billy went on to describe how we are separated from God because of sin in our lives. "Sin" is the wrong we think, feel, and do in our lives. "Sin" is not being perfect and holy as we measure ourselves against a perfect and holy God. In another verse in the Bible it says, "For the wages of sin is death, but the free gift of God is eternal life through Christ Jesus our Lord." The "wages" or the cost of sin is "death." This "death" is the death of our relationship or connection with God. It is a separation from God. It has resulted in a lack of knowing Him and knowing His love for us.

God so loves you and me that He sent His one and only Son to mend this relationship through His death. Jesus paid the "wage" for our sin. He paid the penalty for our sins so that they would be forgiven and we then could know God and his love for us, and be with Him forever.

When Billy Graham told us in the audience sitting in County Stadium (where the Milwaukee Brewers used to play) so many years ago that God loved each of us and He sent his Son to mend our relationship with Him, I felt like he was talking directly to me. He described the truth that Jesus died on the cross to pay the penalty (or wages) for my sins, and what I needed to do was to believe in Him, to put my faith in Him, to trust in Him to save me through what He did for me. Way back then, as a teenager, I put my faith in Jesus as my personal Savior—He saved me from eternal separation from God and brought me into a relationship with Him that started that day and continues to this day. And I know it will last forever.

What Jesus did for me, He wants to do for you. He wants to save you and give you the free gift of eternal life, which is a relationship we enter into with Him that can start today and lasts forever. I would suggest to you to put your name into the verse John 3:16, where it says the word "world," because it is true—God so loves you.

To understand His love for each of us and the difference He wants to make in our lives, take some time to work through the pages of this short book. Go through it with a friend, a family member, a co-worker, someone you feel comfortable enough with to open your heart and mind to and to talk about what just might become the most important part of your life—to know God and to be known by Him.

We begin by unpacking the story that surrounds that famous verse—John 3:16. Turn to chapter one of *John, Jesus, & Me*, and let's begin a journey together through the Gospel of John, talking about Jesus, and sharing with each other what is happening in our own lives. Let's have a conversation about the gospel of John, the Messiah Jesus, and you and me.

CHAPTER 1

THE GIFT OF ETERNITY

John 3:1-21

It was a cool, calm spring night. Jesus had found a quiet place to sit with some of His disciples, His devoted followers, around a fire in the heart of Jerusalem. Many Jews from all over the Roman world had made their way there to celebrate the Passover to remember how God had rescued them from their slavery in Egypt so many centuries earlier. The daylight hours were abuzz with activity, but now that it was night, things had quieted down. It was *this* night though, at the beginning of the public ministry of Jesus, when things were about to get interesting. The key that unlocked the door to eternal life was going to be revealed.

Jesus and His followers saw a man coming to them from the shadows.

> [1] There was a man named Nicodemus, a Jewish religious leader who was a Pharisee. [2] After dark one evening, he came to speak with Jesus. "Rabbi," he said, "we all know that God has sent you to teach us. Your miraculous signs are evidence that God is with you." (John 3:1-2)

Jesus knew why Nicodemus was there. It seemed like He also knew He didn't have a lot of time to talk so He dove right into the heart of the matter.

³ Jesus replied, "I tell you the truth, unless you are born again, you cannot see the Kingdom of God." (John 3:3)

The reality is, to be in the kingdom with the Lord, to live with the Lord forever in His paradise, Nicodemus had to be born again. What was true for Nicodemus is still true for us today.

For a "kingdom" to be a reality you need a ruler, a place for the ruler to rule, and a people to rule over. In this future kingdom that Jesus said we may one day see, who will be the ruler, where is the place He will rule, and who are the people He will rule over?

_____

_____

_____

_____

_____

_____

Nicodemus was one of the smartest men in Jerusalem in that day and he struggled to grasp this truth.

⁴ "What do you mean?" exclaimed Nicodemus. "How can an old man go back into his mother's womb and be born again?" ⁵ Jesus replied, "I assure you, no one can enter the Kingdom of God without being born of water and the Spirit. ⁶ Humans can reproduce only human life, but the Holy Spirit gives birth to spiritual life." (John 3:4-6)

In order to see the kingdom of God, which means we go to heaven when we die and spend an eternity with the Lord, we have to be born once physically and then born again spiritually. God brings about the miracle of physical birth when a baby is formed in the womb and is born. Then He brings about the miracle of spiritual birth when a person is born a second time—born from above. God the Holy Spirit comes into our hearts and resides there, guaranteeing that we will be with Him for eternity.

God living in us . . . let that sink in. Being born again is to have a new life where the God who created the universe comes to live within us. Why would that concept be hard to accept?

_____

_____

_____

_____

_____

_____

I can imagine, as Jesus and Nicodemus were talking with His disciples listening in, a breeze kicked up and Jesus seized the moment to tell Nicodemus more about this truth.

> [7] "So don't be surprised when I say, 'You must be born again.' [8] The wind blows wherever it wants. Just as you can hear the wind but can't tell where it comes from or where it is going, so you can't explain how people are born of the Spirit." (John 3:7-8)

This concept of being born again is mysterious. We cannot see the Holy Spirit, just like we cannot see the wind. But, as surely as the wind moves the leaves on the trees and makes the waves form on the water, so too the Holy Spirit of God has the power to make a difference in our lives.

Jesus was talking about being born again, or born of the Spirit. Look up these verses to see how the Holy Spirit works in our lives (John 14:16-17, 25-26; 15:26; 16:5-15). Given what you just read, how can the Holy Spirit make a difference in our lives?

_____

_____

_____

_____

_____

⁹ "How are these things possible?" Nicodemus asked. ¹⁰ Jesus replied, "You are a respected Jewish teacher, and yet you don't understand these things? ¹¹ I assure you, we tell you what we know and have seen, and yet you won't believe our testimony. ¹² But if you don't believe me when I tell you about earthly things, how can you possibly believe if I tell you about heavenly things? ¹³ No one has ever gone to heaven and returned. But the Son of Man has come down from heaven." (John 3:9-13)

In that last sentence, Jesus was speaking about Himself. He left His throne in heaven above with God the Father to physically live on this earth below for the sole purpose of securing our eternity for us.

¹⁴ "And as Moses lifted up the bronze snake on a pole in the wilderness, so the Son of Man must be lifted up, ¹⁵ so that everyone who believes in him will have eternal life. ¹⁶ For this is how God loved the world: He gave his one and only Son, so that everyone who believes in him will not perish but have eternal life. ¹⁷ God sent his Son into the world not to judge the world, but to save the world through him." (John 3:14-17)

Given what Jesus said in John 3:14-17, is every person in the world "saveable" or able to be saved and spend eternal life with God? Explain.

_____

_____

_____

_____

_____

There was a sergeant in the Polish Army during World War II. His name was Franciszek Gajowniczek (*I know, I can't pronounce it either*). He was captured by the Nazis and brought to the Auschwitz Concentration Camp in 1940. While there he met another prisoner, Maximillian Kolbe. Maximillian was a Catholic Priest. In the summer of 1941 a prisoner escaped from the camp. Karl Fritsch, the Nazi officer in charge of that block of prisoners ordered all the other prisoners to come out and line up. He announced that a prisoner had escaped. To pay for his escape he would choose ten other prisoners randomly to die of starvation, "When I call your number, you will step forward." Fritsch started to draw numbers while the prisoners stared at their forearms where their numbers had been tattooed onto them. Then he called, "5659." It was Franciszek's number. He stepped forward and dropped to his knees in front of the Nazi soldiers and pleaded for his life, "I have a family. Please do not choose me." Just then, another man made his way through the prisoners, "I am a Catholic priest from Poland; I would like to take his place, because he has a wife and children." It was Maximillian Kolbe. In a rare act of twisted mercy, Fritsch allowed Maximillian to take the place of Franciszek. After being taken with the nine other prisoners to a dungeon and starved of all food and water, on August 14, 1941, Maximillian Kolbe died in Franciszek Gajowniczek's place. Franciszek went on to live out his years in Poland and died on March 13, 1995. He was 93.

A man choosing to die in the place of another is the picture of what Jesus did for us. When Jesus said, "as Moses lifted up the bronze snake on a pole in the wilderness, so the Son of Man must be lifted up," He was speaking about His own death—being lifted up on a cross. Jesus was crucified on a cross in our place. He died for you and me. He took our penalty. He took our punishment for our sins. He took the wrath and judgment of God against our sin upon Himself so that we might live forever with Him. He died so we could see His kingdom and be with Him for all of eternity.

There are three aspects to this eternal life and all have to do with a relationship with God. First, we enter into this relationship by being born again (John 3:3). Second, we grow in this relationship with God by investing our lives into it just like we would grow in any relationship. And third, this relationship is eternal. Once each of us believes that Jesus died to pay our penalty for our sins He sends the Holy Spirit into us. And when we have the Holy Spirit in us we are guaranteed that we will be with God forever. God's judgment against our sins is lifted and our relationship with Him has been mended.

> [18] "There is no judgment against anyone who believes in him. But anyone who does not believe in him has already been judged for not believing in God's one and only Son." (John 3:18)

Why is it so hard for us to believe and come into the light of Jesus? Jesus describes why.

> [19] "And the judgment is based on this fact: God's light came into the world, but people loved the darkness more than the light, for their actions were evil. [20] All who do evil hate the light and refuse to go near it for fear their sins will be exposed." (John 3:19-20)

What stops people from coming into the light that Jesus offers according to John 3:19-20?

_____

_____

_____

---

²¹ "But those who do what is right come to the light so others can see that they are doing what God wants." (John 3:21)

After we enter this relationship with Jesus, in order to grow in it we commit ourselves to living in His truth as it is laid out in the Bible. To live with the Lord today we commit our lives to Him and desire for Him to shine through us. Then, those words will ring true of our lives, "so others can see that they are doing what God wants." In other words, we would be living our lives in God's light.

Who gets to decide what the truth is? How do we live in the truth? Jesus said of Himself, "I am the way, the *truth*, and the life." He told us the truth about eternity. He brings us into this eternity and guarantees it by sending the Holy Spirit to live within us. There is no greater news in the entire universe than this! If you have not come into the Light of Jesus, won't you believe in Him alone to save you?

Have you believed that Jesus is God and was lifted up on the cross to pay the penalty for your sins? Have you trusted in Jesus alone to save you from that penalty and give you the gift of eternal life? Have you placed your faith in Jesus to have this eternal relationship with Him?

Yes: _____ No: _____ I'm still thinking about it: _____

CHAPTER 2

DRINK THE WATER

John 4:1-26

We need water. Without it we would only last a week. Our bodies are made up of about 60% water. Our brains are about 70% water and our lungs are almost 90% water. If we stop drinking water we will begin to feel clumsy and exhausted. Then, if we continue to avoid fluids, our eyesight will start to go, followed by vomiting, and finally we will slip into a coma and . . . well, you can guess what comes next. Naturally, we won't allow ourselves to be thirsty for too long. As soon as we start to feel dehydrated we will quickly track down some fluids to satisfy our parched cravings.

Was there ever a time when you were extremely thirsty or dehydrated? What was the scenario, and what did it feel like? How may that help us picture what people feel like being spiritually dehydrated?

_____

_____

_____

John, Jesus, & Me

The next chapter we are looking at in the gospel of John begins with Jesus heading north out of Judea toward the Sea of Galilee. He knew He needed to go and talk to a woman who was spiritually dehydrated. About halfway between the Dead Sea and the Sea of Galilee, His disciples and He stopped to take a break in Samaria, a land that was hostile toward Jews.

> [1] Jesus knew the Pharisees had heard that he was baptizing and making more disciples than John [2] (though Jesus himself didn't baptize them—his disciples did). [3] So he left Judea and returned to Galilee.
>
> [4] He had to go through Samaria on the way. [5] Eventually he came to the Samaritan village of Sychar, near the field that Jacob gave to his son Joseph. [6] Jacob's well was there; and Jesus, tired from the long walk, sat wearily beside the well about noontime. (John 4:1-6)

It was hot and dry with the sun beating down and Jesus knew He needed to be there. So He sat and waited . . . until He saw her coming. She walked toward Him, coming to the well by herself to get water. This was not the normal practice of the women who lived in Sychar. Coming alone probably meant this Samaritan woman who would encounter Jesus was an outcast among the other women in her hometown.

> [7] Soon a Samaritan woman came to draw water, and Jesus said to her, "Please give me a drink." [8] He was alone at the time because his disciples had gone into the village to buy some food.
>
> [9] The woman was surprised, for Jews refuse to have anything to do with Samaritans. She said to Jesus, "You are a Jew, and I am a Samaritan woman. Why are you asking me for a drink?"
>
> [10] Jesus replied, "If you only knew the gift God has for you and who you are speaking to, you would ask me, and I would give you living water." (John 4:7-10)

Jesus was offering this woman a gift—"the gift God has for you," and it is a gift God has for you and me. Give your best definition of a gift?

_____

_____

_____

_____

When Jesus said "living water" in that day it was the same thing as saying "flowing water." If we look down into a well, we will see water under the ground that actually flows like an underground river. So the woman naturally thought on a physical plane when she responded to what Jesus said.

> [11] "But sir, you don't have a rope or a bucket," she said, "and this well is very deep. Where would you get this living water? [12] And besides, do you think you're greater than our ancestor Jacob, who gave us this well? How can you offer better water than he and his sons and his animals enjoyed?" (John 4:11-12)

Oh, if she only knew how much greater Jesus was than Jacob! The water Jesus offered was so different than physical water, which quenches thirsty bodies. The water Jesus offered was to quench her thirsty soul.

> [13] Jesus replied, "Anyone who drinks this water will soon become thirsty again. [14] But those who drink the water I give will never be thirsty again. It becomes a fresh, bubbling spring within them, giving them eternal life." (John 4:13-14)

What an amazing offer! There has never been an offer like this before. No matter what people go after to satisfy the thirst in their hearts, like love, success, wealth, fame, or countless other wells people drink from, when they rise from them they find they have no lasting inward satisfaction, no enduring fulfillment. To stay alive physically you have to continue to drink water. To be alive spiritually you only have to drink the water Jesus offers once. This was the truth Jesus gave to the woman he encountered at that well. What Jesus told the woman then, He tells us today:

> ¹⁴ "But those who drink the water I give will never be thirsty again. It becomes a fresh, bubbling spring within them, giving them eternal life." (John 4:14)

When I read, "It becomes a fresh, bubbling spring within them," I picture shining a light down the well of a person's heart and seeing that it is bone dry before receiving the gift of this living water. People have thrown their own buckets of water down there, for they try to quench their thirst with their work, other people, alcohol, you name it; but their soul remains dry. Then, when a person receives the living water Jesus offers, the flowing water is clearly seen. Looking down into the well of their heart we see new life sparkling down there, never to go dry again! As this new Christian grows in their relationship with the Lord the spring of living water continues to bubble up, filling the well of their soul.

> ¹⁵ "Please, sir," the woman said, "give me this water! Then I'll never be thirsty again, and I won't have to come here to get water."
>
> ¹⁶ "Go and get your husband," Jesus told her.
>
> ¹⁷ "I don't have a husband," the woman replied.
>
> Jesus said, "You're right! You don't have a husband—¹⁸ for you have had five husbands, and you aren't even married to the man you're living with now. You certainly spoke the truth!"
>
> ¹⁹ "Sir," the woman said, "you must be a prophet." (John 4:15-19)

The woman wanted to talk about actual H_2O (John 4:11 & 15), but Jesus wanted to talk about living water (John 4:10 & 13-14). How about you? Being sincere in your reflection, what have you been throwing down the well of your soul to try and quench your spiritual thirst?

_____

_____

_____

Who do you know needs "a fresh, bubbling spring within them"? Do you think Jesus is the only one who can satisfy a thirsty soul? Why or why not?

_____

_____

_____

Let me "translate" that last quote of the woman, "Okay, I am freaking out that you know all this about me!" It would be best to interpret what she said this way, *"Ah, um, I can't believe you know me. We've never met, but You are right about my broken heart. I've given up on love. I'm really just surviving, existing. My soul, my heart, is barren, dry. I am oh so thirsty. How did you know?"*

Jesus opened her heart up to talk about what she really longed for. It is what we all, deep down inside, long for—a relationship with God. The woman continued,

> [20] "So tell me, why is it that you Jews insist that Jerusalem is the only place of worship, while we Samaritans claim it is here at Mount Gerizim, where our ancestors worshiped?"

²¹ Jesus replied, "Believe me, dear woman, the time is coming when it will no longer matter whether you worship the Father on this mountain or in Jerusalem. ²² You Samaritans know very little about the one you worship, while we Jews know all about him, for salvation comes through the Jews. ²³ But the time is coming—indeed it's here now—when true worshipers will worship the Father in spirit and in truth. The Father is looking for those who will worship him that way. ²⁴ For God is Spirit, so those who worship him must worship in spirit and in truth." (John 4:20-24)

She thought God wanted people to practice religion, recite platitudes, and perform rituals. Jesus could now talk to her about being a true worshiper of God. He could talk to her about how to connect with God and truly honor Him. He talked to her about how this living water could spring up in her.

> In your mind, what do "true worshipers" of God do? What do you think Jesus meant when He said, "those who worship [God] must worship in spirit and truth"? Just think about what the words "worship," "spirit," and "truth" mean? How can we be sure we are true worshipers (vs. false worshipers)?
>
> _____
>
> _____
>
> _____

Clearly the words of Jesus made perfect sense to the woman. She could tell He spoke with authority and she began to wonder about Him.

²⁵ The woman said, "I know the Messiah is coming—the one who is called Christ. When he comes, he will explain everything to us."

²⁶ Then Jesus told her, "I Am the Messiah!" (John 4:25-26)

A monumental declaration, an eternal revelation! Jesus brought her to the point where she needed to trust that He was the Messiah. The Messiah meant Jesus is the One appointed by God to rescue people from being separated from God and to bring them to be with Him forever. Jesus was the One who had come to save her and to give her living water springing up to eternal life!

The offer of living water is the Christian gospel—the good news that Jesus came to die to pay the penalty for our sins and make us right before God our Father. He rose from the grave to give us an eternal relationship with Him. He lives to quench our thirsty souls. To drink the living water is to receive the gift of eternal life—a relationship with Jesus that starts today and lasts forever. Once each of us receives this gift we will never have the well of our souls be dry again.

Are you spiritually thirsty? Explain. Have you turned to Jesus to quench your thirsty soul? Why or why not?

_____

_____

_____

_____

CHAPTER 3

EAT THE BREAD

John 6:19-40

Bread is as old as written history. We can go all the way back into ancient Egypt and find that people baked bread. In the ministry of Jesus, He mentioned bread often. Jesus included bread in the Lord's Prayer when He said, "give us this day our daily bread"[1] (Matthew 6:11; Luke 11:3). He talked about bread with yeast which spread throughout it (Matthew 13:33; Luke 13:21). He instituted communion as He broke bread (Matthew 26:26; Mark 14:22; Luke 22:19). After He rose from the dead, Jesus talked to two men as they walked on the road to the town of Emmaus and then ate bread with them (Luke 24:30). Soon after that, Jesus baked bread for His disciples on the shore of the sea (John 21:9).

Probably the most memorable time Jesus used bread was when a boy was found with his lunch, which consisted of five small loaves of bread made out of barley, along with two fish. When Jesus was up near the Sea of Galilee a large crowd followed Him because they saw Him perform many miracles as He healed the sick. Jesus had the crowd sit down on the side of the mountain and asked His disciples how they were going to feed all those people (about

---

[1]   From the New American Standard Bible (NASB) version.

21

five-thousand men along with women and children). The disciples of Jesus gave a number of different answers, but it was one of His disciples, Andrew, who brought to Jesus this small lunch from that little boy. Jesus took the loaves and fish, gave thanks and had His disciples distribute the food. In the end, by the miracle of Jesus, everyone had as much as they wanted with twelve baskets full of leftovers.[2]

Because of that miracle, the crowd wanted to take Jesus by force and make Him king, but He withdrew to a mountain by Himself. In the meantime, as it was getting late, His disciples got into a boat to go to Capernaum on the northwest side of the Sea of Galilee. On their way, the sea began to stir as the winds blew. The disciples were getting nowhere. Then, they saw Jesus and did not recognize Him as He walked on the water toward them. They were frightened for they thought He was a ghost!

> [19] They had rowed three or four miles when suddenly they saw Jesus walking on the water toward the boat. They were terrified, [20] but he called out to them, "Don't be afraid. I am here!" [21] Then they were eager to let him in the boat, and immediately they arrived at their destination!

> [22] The next day the crowd that had stayed on the far shore saw that the disciples had taken the only boat, and they realized Jesus had not gone with them. [23] Several boats from Tiberias landed near the place where the Lord had blessed the bread and the people had eaten. [24] So when the crowd saw that neither Jesus nor his disciples were there, they got into the boats and went across to Capernaum to look for him. [25] They found him on the other side of the lake and asked, "Rabbi, when did you get here?" (John 6:19-25)

It was at that moment Jesus was going to use bread to teach one of the most profound spiritual truths. Let's find out what that is as we walk through the rest of this passage in John 6.

---

[2] John 6:1-14

²⁶ Jesus replied, "I tell you the truth, you want to be with me because I fed you, not because you understood the miraculous signs." (John 6:26)

The warning Jesus was making here was against a pursuit of a relationship with Him for material gain, for a miracle, or to have their stomachs filled. He warned against their self-centered search of Him and ours today. Here is how it can show up in our thinking, "I will seek to know Jesus so I will have an easy life; so He will ensure I have food on the table; so I'll get my fill of health, wealth, and happiness." It is a pursuit of Jesus because "I want Jesus to make me feel good." This is spiritual bread full of empty carbs and it does not last. If the crowd got that from Jesus it would taste good for a while, but it would not stick. They would quickly become spiritually hungry again. It is the same for you and me.

> This is a good time to check our motives. Think through why you follow Jesus, or why you *would* follow Jesus. After writing your reasons down determine if it is for "spiritual bread full of empty carbs" and explain why or why not.
>
> _____
>
> _____
>
> _____
>
> _____

Jesus goes on and says,

²⁷ But don't be so concerned about perishable things like food. (John 6:27a)

Jesus is not encouraging us to be out of touch with tangible things like what we should eat. What He is saying is when we work for bread that lacks nutrition (pursuing whatever it is for earthly gains), it ultimately turns out like moldy bread—it perishes.

Butler Road '55 t '65   1958

When my dad was in high school, his parents (my grandpa and grandma) opened up "Vance Frozen Custards" in New Castle, Pennsylvania. It was a great idea before its time. People loved it! Today, Vance Frozen Custards is no more. My Grandma and Grandpa closed the doors in 1965. Vance Frozen Custards stand did not last. You might remember E.F. Hutton. Their slogan was, "When E.F. Hutton talks – people listen." He stopped talking—the company no longer exists. How about Woolworth's (five and dime store)? They opened in 1879. By 1997 all the stores were closed. The DeLorean Motor Company produced the DeLorean car that the movie "Back to the Future" made famous. The company started in 1975 and by 1982 they claimed bankruptcy. These companies and many more were great ideas and great businesses, but ultimately that *bread* ended up perishing.

There is nothing wrong with pursuing a profession. There is honor in getting an education. Whether you own a business or work for one, investing our energy in work is commendable in the eyes of the Lord.[3] When Jesus said, "don't be so concerned about perishable things like food," (John 6:27a) He was guiding us to put things into their proper perspective and to always know the things of this world will eventually wear out. Even pursuing a relationship with Jesus for gain in this world, like the crowd was doing, is like eating empty carbs—it will not have lasting satisfaction. So, work for things that will never perish. Or, to continue the metaphor of Jesus, eat the bread that is nutritious!

> [27] "But don't be so concerned about perishable things like food. Spend your energy seeking the eternal life that the Son of Man can give you. For God the Father has given me the seal of his approval." (John 6:27)

Remember, "eternal life" is a relationship we have with the Lord that we enter into when we are born again. Yet, like in any relationship, we grow in this eternal life when we invest in it. That is why Jesus said, "Spend your energy seeking the eternal life that the Son of Man can give you." Jesus is talking about putting our energies into our relationship with Him.

> [28] They replied, "We want to perform God's works, too. What should we do?" (John 6:28)

That is such a common response! "What should I do to do what God wants? What should I do to show God I am worthy of His goodness? What should I do to invest in this relationship? Should I say certain prayers, chant certain things, behave in certain ways?" The way we go about eating the bread that is nutritious is by doing nothing except believing in Jesus.

> [29] Jesus told them, "This is the only work God wants from you: Believe in the one he has sent." (John 6:29)

Once we have trusted that Jesus is our only hope to get right with or be accepted by God the Father because He died on the cross to pay

---

[3]   Ecclesiastes 5:18; 1 Thessalonians 4:11

for our sins, then we can grow in this relationship only through faith also. To believe is not just to agree with the facts, like saying, "Yes, I believe in Jesus." To believe is to have a humble dependence on Jesus. Believing in Jesus is having a need for Him always—every moment of every day. To believe in Him daily means we rely on Him for wisdom, for our spiritual growth, for our wellbeing, for our strength, etc. It is a calling out to Him to give us His strength to say "no" to sin in our lives and to rescue us from the influences all around us that pull us away from Him. To believe is to trust more in Him and less in ourselves. To believe in Jesus means He increases and you and I decrease in importance in our lives. The nutritious food that endures to eternal life is bread that is all about relying on Jesus. Therefore, we have the mentality, "I am doing this (whatever it may be) because God is desiring it for me and I want to do His work by the strength He provides. I want to walk with Him by faith, trusting Him as I go along in life."

In John 6:28-29 Jesus clarifies how we are to do the work of God. Given the understanding of "believe" in the paragraph above, how have you believed in Jesus lately?

_____

_____

_____

Let's continue with the interaction between Jesus and those He gave the bread to and dive into the truth He was imparting to them.

³⁰ They answered, "Show us a miraculous sign if you want us to believe in you. What can you do? ³¹ After all, our ancestors ate manna while they journeyed through the wilderness! The Scriptures say, 'Moses gave them bread from heaven to eat.'"

³² Jesus said, "I tell you the truth, Moses didn't give you bread from heaven. My Father did. And now he offers you the true

bread from heaven. ³³ The true bread of God is the one who comes down from heaven and gives life to the world." (John 6:30-33)

Jesus is the nutrition we need to experience "life." Jesus was sent from the Father in heaven and came to this earth to give us this life.

³⁴ "Sir," they said, "give us that bread every day."

³⁵ Jesus replied, "I am the bread of life. Whoever comes to me will never be hungry again. Whoever believes in me will never be thirsty." (John 6:34-35)

Jesus clearly said it, "I am the bread of life." And with that statement, Jesus lays out four nutritious ingredients we get from Him to experience this "life" He is talking about, an abundant life which He desires for us. The first ingredient in Jesus is our eternal satisfaction. Let's read those words of Jesus again in John 6:35.

³⁵ Jesus replied, "I am the bread of life. Whoever comes to me will never be hungry again. Whoever believes in me will never be thirsty." (John 6:35)

Did you catch that word, "never"? "Never" means never. No room is left for spiritual hunger and thirst after coming to Jesus and believing in Him. This does not exclude a desire to grow and mature in our relationship with the Lord. However, this word, "never," rules out forever the possibility of an unsatisfied hunger. When you and I have Jesus in our lives the void in our souls—the spiritual hunger—is filled.

³⁶ "But you haven't believed in me even though you have seen me." (John 6:36)

As a side note, Jesus gives a warning with this verse. All along Jesus has been clarifying how He is the nutritious bread that we must dine on, and then there is this interjection here. In this verse, Jesus explains how faith and knowing that we are getting the nutrition we need from Jesus works. His followers were saying, show us a sign and we will believe (verse 30). That's not how it works. It is not, "If we see what Jesus is doing we will believe."[4] It is, "We believe and therefore we see that Jesus is all that we need."

Believing, or faith, is having a conviction or being convinced that something is true when we do not see it.[5] First we turn to Jesus and believe in Him to rescue us from the penalty of our sins. He died on the cross to take our punishment so that we can be saved from it and the eternal condemnation that is a result of our sin. When we place our faith in Jesus He sends the Holy Spirit to live in us—that is what it means to be born again. It is at that moment that we enter into an eternal relationship with the Lord. From that moment on we can continue to invest and grow in our relationship with Him. The way we do that is the same way we started into this relationship—by faith. When we trust Him in all aspects of our lives, *then* we will see Him actively working in our lives. When we trust in Him in the present tense (right now) we see He saves us from the power of sin in our lives, molds us into His image, comforts us, guides us, gives us hope for our eternity with Him, and all the things that the Bible lays out regarding our relationship with Him. This is the delicious ingredient of eternal satisfaction.

It looks like John 6:36 is a reprimand from Jesus. Here, Jesus was saying, 'You have even seen Me and the miracles I've done, and yet you do not believe?' How have you seen Jesus lately by believing in Him? (Hint: How have you seen Him bring victory; or physical, emotional, or spiritual health; or conviction, comfort, wisdom, etc., in your life?)

_____

_____

_____

---

[4] *They saw Jesus right in front of them walking on the water!*

[5] Hebrews 11:1

The second of four nutritious ingredients we receive through Jesus is eternal security.

> [37] "However, those the Father has given me will come to me, and I will never reject them. [38] For I have come down from heaven to do the will of God who sent me, not to do my own will. [39] And this is the will of God, that I should not lose even one of all those he has given me," (John 6:37-39a)

It is a comfort to know that no matter who we are or what our background is, if we come to Jesus we will not be rejected. Jesus will "not lose even one of all those he has given me"—no one! Once you and I are saved, we can never become unsaved!

What might make us feel uncertain about being sure we will be in heaven with Jesus when we die?

_____

_____

_____

Many Christians, I'm afraid, feel uncertain about their eternal life. They feel like a burglar can come and steal their salvation. They may be insecure that they have too much sin, not enough faith, or too many doubts or failures. The Lord wants us to feast on this truth: when we are in Jesus, when we have placed our faith in Him for eternal life, we will never be cast out from Him—never! Nothing can separate us from the Lord when we are in Jesus, when we are born again,[6] when we are Christians. Nothing!

Those who are in Jesus have eternal satisfaction, eternal security, and the third of four ingredients we enjoy in Jesus is an eternal hope.

---

[6]   Remember Chapter 1 and the interaction with Nicodemus.

³⁹ "And this is the will of God, that I should not lose even one of all those he has given me, but that I should raise them up at the last day. ⁴⁰ For it is my Father's will that all who see his Son and believe in him should have eternal life. I will raise them up at the last day." (John 6:39-40)

The Lord Jesus will raise us up on the last day. There is coming a "last day." Let me try and summarize what that last day will look like. There will come a day when the Lord Jesus will descend from heaven and bring Christians up to be with Him in heaven. In Christian circles, it is typically called "the rapture." We will meet Jesus in the clouds and be with Him forever in His paradise.[7] No matter how hopeless life may feel, we have a hope and a future with the Lord, for we know we will spend forever with Him!

> Hope is a positively powerful feeling or desire. How can hoping for or looking forward to your eternity with the Lord be a positive influence in your life?
>
> _____
>
> _____
>
> _____
>
> _____

The first three healthy ingredients that we dine on when we have Jesus are eternal satisfaction, eternal security, and eternal hope. The final healthy ingredient we have in Jesus is eternal companionship.

⁴⁰ "For it is my Father's will that all who see his Son and believe in him should have eternal life." (John 6:40)[8]

---

[7] 1 Thessalonians 4:13-18

[8] Jesus mentions this "eternal life" three other times in this passage: John 6:27, 47, 54

The reality is, everyone will have an eternal life. The question is, will each of us live this eternal life with or without Jesus? In another passage in the New Testament the Apostle Paul wrote these words, "And this is the secret: Christ lives in you. This gives you assurance of sharing his glory." (Colossians 1:27). When the Holy Spirit is in us God is in us. This means Jesus Christ is in us. With Christ in us we can have companionship with Him and a partnership with Him as our "bread of life." This eternal life is where we live with and for Him today and forever.

I love bread. There is a lot of bread out there that tastes so good, but it lacks nutrition. If we want to be healthy deep in our souls, the only spiritually nutritious bread is Jesus. He taught us here in John 6 that we are to believe in Him for our satisfaction, security, hope and companionship. It is our Lord's desire that every person will come to love Him as the bread of their life, for He is the only One who gives the gift of eternal life.[9]

In John 17:3, Jesus defined eternal life. He said, "This is eternal life, that they may know You, the only true God, and Jesus Christ whom You have sent." (NASB version) Eternal life is a relationship with God that starts today and lasts forever. Given what you just went through in this chapter, how are you certain that you have entered into a relationship with God? How have you been trusting and growing in your relationship with Him lately?

_____

_____

_____

_____

---

[9]   1 Timothy 2:3-6

CHAPTER 4

WHY ME?

John 9:1-41

Each one of us has a unique story to tell. Some of us feel pretty good about our story while others feel ashamed. Some of us have had it pretty easy while others have been through the wringer. Have you ever reflected on your life and thought, "Why me?" "Why was I born into the family I was born into?" "Why did I grow up in the part of the world I grew up in?" "Why do I have the ethnicity I have?" "Why do I have the disability I have?" "Why was I adopted instead of staying in the family of my biological roots?" "Why is my life such a struggle when others seem to have it so easy?" "Why do I have what I have and others do not?" "Why haven't I had any tragedies in my life?" "Why was I born into wealth?" "Why do I have the life I have through no choice of my own?"

Take a moment and reflect on your life. Write down a bit of your story—what makes your life unique. How might you answer that question, "Why me?"

_____

_____

_____

In John 9 we are introduced to a man whose story could easily be defined by, "Life is not fair. Why me? Why have I had to live this life?" Let me introduce you to him, and as we dig into his story we are going to see why each of us has been given our own stories to tell.

> ¹As Jesus was walking along, he saw a man who had been blind from birth. (John 9:1)

There is a lot packed into those opening words. Here is a guy who had been blind his whole life. In that day (the first century A.D.) it would mean he would be the poorest of the poor. He was a beggar. When people walked by him, no doubt, they would say in their hearts, "I am glad I'm not him."

If someone had a "right" to say, "Why me?" it was this blind man. However, he was not the one who asked Jesus why he was born blind, it was the disciples of Jesus.

> ²"Rabbi, [which means, teacher]" his disciples asked him, "why was this man born blind? Was it because of his own sins or his parents' sins?" (John 9:2)

This was a common thought of that day, assuming someone had sinned to cause a disability. But look at Jesus' response.

> ³"It was not because of his sins or his parents' sins," Jesus answered. "This happened so the power of God could be seen in him. (John 9:3)

Have you ever wondered why God has some people who are born with a disability? Have you ever wondered if it is a punishment from God? What would make it hard to accept the reason Jesus gave for why people are born with disabilities?

_____

_____

_____

The Lord desires to show His mighty works through disabilities.[10] Throughout church history, God has used people with disabilities and hardships to show His mighty works. You and I may ask, "Why me?" and the answer is, "Because, God wants to show His mighty works through us." He may choose not to change our circumstances and show His mighty works through our struggles. Look at the mighty work Jesus decided to do through this man born blind. The next verses start with Jesus speaking,

[4] "We must quickly carry out the tasks assigned us by the one who sent us. The night is coming, and then no one can work. [5] But while I am here in the world, I am the light of the world."

[6] Then he spit on the ground, made mud with the saliva, and spread the mud over the blind man's eyes. [7] He told him, "Go wash yourself in the pool of Siloam" (Siloam means "sent"). So the man went and washed and came back seeing!

[8] His neighbors and others who knew him as a blind beggar asked each other, "Isn't this the man who used to sit and beg?" [9] Some said he was, and others said, "No, he just looks like him!"

But the beggar kept saying, "Yes, I am the same one!"

[10] They asked, "Who healed you? What happened?"

[11] He told them, "The man they call Jesus made mud and spread it over my eyes and told me, 'Go to the pool of Siloam and wash yourself.' So I went and washed, and now I can see!"

[12] "Where is he now?" they asked.

"I don't know," he replied.

---

[10] For instance, Moses had a speech impediment, but God used him to be one of the greatest leaders in world history. The Apostle Paul had a thorn in his flesh. Some scholars speculate it could have been poor eyesight. Yet, God used Him to start and strengthen churches all over the known world in the first century.

¹³ Then they took the man who had been blind to the Pharisees, ¹⁴ because it was on the Sabbath that Jesus had made the mud and healed him. ¹⁵ The Pharisees asked the man all about it. So he told them, "He put the mud over my eyes, and when I washed it away, I could see!"

¹⁶ Some of the Pharisees said, "This man Jesus is not from God, for he is working on the Sabbath." Others said, "But how could an ordinary sinner do such miraculous signs?" So there was a deep division of opinion among them. (John 9:4-16)

Instead of seeing the miracle that took place, the Pharisees, the religious leaders of the day, were trying to find fault with the One who had performed it.

> Stop a moment and reflect on the Lord's mighty hand in your life. How have you seen Him actively working? Think of ways He has (or probably has) made a difference in your life, the gifts He has given to you, and the ways He has had an impact on you (and you may not have even acknowledged it before).
>
> _____
>
> _____
>
> _____
>
> _____

Let's pick up the story of the blind man where we left off.

¹⁷ Then the Pharisees again questioned the man who had been blind and demanded, "What's your opinion about this man who healed you?" The man replied, "I think he must be a prophet."

> ¹⁸ The Jewish leaders still refused to believe the man had been blind and could now see, so they called in his parents. ¹⁹ They asked them, "Is this your son? Was he born blind? If so, how can he now see?"
>
> ²⁰ His parents replied, "We know this is our son and that he was born blind, ²¹ but we don't know how he can see or who healed him. Ask him. He is old enough to speak for himself." ²² His parents said this because they were afraid of the Jewish leaders, who had announced that anyone saying Jesus was the Messiah would be expelled from the synagogue. ²³ That's why they said, "He is old enough. Ask him." (John 9:17-23)

I imagine this couple had worked really hard to be accepted and to remove the stigma of having a child like their son. The common wisdom of their day was that if a child was born with a disability it was because of the sins of the parents (remember the question from the disciples above?). The text above seems to hint at the fact that the parents had faith in Jesus as the Messiah, but fear was dominating them. The fear we struggle with is the same one the man's parents had, the fear of rejection. Perhaps we are reluctant to share how Jesus has made a difference in our lives because we fear being outcasts with our peers, our coworkers, or even our families.

Jesus wants us to be governed by faith, not fear. Look how this young man had a courageous faith.

> ²⁴ So for the second time they called in the man who had been blind and told him, "God should get the glory for this, because we know this man Jesus is a sinner."
>
> ²⁵ "I don't know whether he is a sinner," the man replied. "But I know this: I was blind, and now I can see!" (John 9:24-25)

How the man responded has to be my favorite quote of the whole passage. *You can call Jesus whatever you want. You can reject Him. All I know is He changed my life.*

> ²⁶ "But what did he do?" they asked. "How did he heal you?"

²⁷ "Look!" the man exclaimed. "I told you once. Didn't you listen? Why do you want to hear it again? Do you want to become his disciples, too?"

²⁸ Then they cursed him and said, "You are his disciple, but we are disciples of Moses! ²⁹ We know God spoke to Moses, but we don't even know where this man comes from."

³⁰ "Why, that's very strange!" the man replied. "He healed my eyes, and yet you don't know where he comes from?" (John 9:26-30)

That guy had guts! He didn't care what those powerful religious leaders thought. He knew Jesus must be from God for He healed him of his blindness.

The parents of the man born blind, who was healed by Jesus, were fearful. Their son displayed courageous faith. When it comes to being bold about what Jesus has done in your life do you tip the scales more toward being governed by fear or by faith? Write out examples in your life when you did what you did because of fear and then do the same for when you acted with courageous faith and think of why either influenced you.

_____

_____

_____

_____

Look what the man born blind said next,

³¹ "We know that God doesn't listen to sinners, but he is ready to hear those who worship him and do his will." (John 9:31)

The man mixed some truth into his statement. As sinners God *does* hear us if we reach out to Him in faith to save us from our sins. That is how we enter into our relationship with Him—by trusting that Jesus died to take our punishment upon Himself for our sins. Here is the truth behind what the man was saying: after we have entered into this relationship with the Lord by becoming born again, if we are going to continue to connect with God on a relational level we must turn away from sin and turn toward Him. James 4:6-10 tells us to humble ourselves in the sight of the Lord and He will lift us up. 1 Peter 3:12 (quoting from Psalm 34), hits the nail on the head that we must be humble before the Lord as we relate to Him. If we are going to follow Jesus we must have a reverence for Him, be obedient to Him, and let people know, "He changed my life!"

On June 4, 1783 in the French village of Annonay, not far from Paris, Joseph and Jacques Montgolfier stoked a smoky bonfire on a raised platform fed by wet straw and old wool rags. Tethered above was a huge silk and paper bag thirty-three feet in diameter. In the presence of a cheering crowd the very first hot air balloon was cut from its moorings and set free to rise majestically into the noon sky. Over 3000 feet into the air it went—the first public ascent of a balloon, the first step in the history of human flight.[11] And as the story goes, it came back to earth, over a mile away in a field, where it was promptly attacked by pitchfork-waving peasants and torn to pieces as an instrument of evil.

When the Lord Jesus changes our lives and lifts us out of our darkness there will always be people who want to attack our relationship with Him. Family members reject us, friends abandon us, and associates discredit us.

---

[11] http://www.britannica.com/EBchecked/topic/1404137/Joseph-Michel-and-Jacques-Etienne-Montgolfier

Have you ever had an experience where "pitchfork wielding" people have attacked you because Jesus changed your life? Write out what happened.

_____

_____

_____

_____

Notice what happened to this man whom Jesus healed. As he was flying high with his new sight and insight on who Jesus was, he said to the Pharisees,

> [32] "Ever since the world began, no one has been able to open the eyes of someone born blind. [33] If this man were not from God, he couldn't have done it."

> [34] "You were born a total sinner!" they answered. "Are you trying to teach us?" And they threw him out of the synagogue. (John 9:32-34)

Power and pride became the means for silencing honesty. People do not want to give up their power, so they will cast out those who identify with the One who has infinite power; the One to Whom we must surrender our power to. Has Jesus changed your life? Don't be afraid to show it—even when people with pitchforks attack us. For we know Jesus is near, just like He was for the seeing blind man.

> [35] When Jesus heard what had happened, he found the man and asked, "Do you believe in the Son of Man?"

> [36] The man answered, "Who is he, sir? I want to believe in him."

³⁷ "You have seen him," Jesus said, "and he is speaking to you!"

³⁸ "Yes, Lord, I believe!" the man said. And he worshiped Jesus. (John 9:35-38)

In John 9:35-38 Jesus found the man and reassured him when he was cast out. Have you ever felt like you were cast out (for example: in school—not being in a certain group, or at work—feeling like an outsider, etc.)? Share a story or two. If you are a Christian, how has Jesus comforted you when others have rejected you?

_____

_____

_____

_____

_____

---

³⁹ Then Jesus told him, "I entered this world to render judgment—to give sight to the blind and to show those who think they see that they are blind." (John 9:39)

Jesus is the perfect judge in order for us to see our sin. He reveals what is right and wrong to us for the sole purpose of saving us from the judgment against our sin. This is called grace!

⁴⁰ Some Pharisees who were standing nearby heard him and asked, "Are you saying we're blind?"

⁴¹ "If you were blind, you wouldn't be guilty," Jesus replied. "But you remain guilty because you claim you can see." (John 9:40-41)

Those who refuse to see their own offenses think they see themselves clearly, but they remain blind. These Pharisees knew the Law. They were bombarded every day with people who broke the Law. Yet, they refused to see their own sins—they thought they saw themselves in truth. The fact was they refused to see they needed Jesus to save them from their sin and guilt.

Every one of our stories is unique. Some of us live with disabilities and ailments. Some go through trials of many kinds, while still others have it pretty easy. No matter your story, Jesus wants to reveal Himself through you and me. When we let Him display Himself through us and tell the world of His wonderful works some will reject us. But Jesus calls us to stay strong in Him. Keep believing in Jesus through it all. And, like the man born blind, when we see Jesus actively working in our lives, let's give Him the worship He deserves.

Jesus masterfully moves from healing physical blindness to speaking about healing spiritual blindness. Are you spiritually blind? Explain. If not, how has Jesus opened your spiritual eyes?

_____

_____

_____

Do you think Jesus wants to open the eyes of the spiritually blind today? How do you think He might use your unique story to open people's eyes to see their need for Him?

_____

_____

_____

CHAPTER 5

WHO IS YOUR SHEPHERD?

John 10:1-10

I've had many people in my life give me guidance. As I grew up my parents showed me the difference between right and wrong, they taught me about hard work and discipline, and what unconditional love looks like. I can remember teachers, coaches, and professors who guided me along the way. Over the years, my wife has shown me how to tangibly love well and lead well. My kids have influenced me to grow in gentleness. The list of people who have guided my life goes on and on.

Share some stories of people in your past who have guided you in your life.

_____

_____

_____

_____

John, Jesus, & Me

We've arrived at John chapter 10. It is important to see the flow from John 9 into John 10. Remember, Jesus healed a man born blind. The man was brought before the religious leaders and questioned. As the interaction escalated he was kicked out of the synagogue which was like being kicked out of the community. Although he was healed, he was like a sheep without a shepherd. Jesus used this analogy to help the people understand what it means to be in God's flock and how they could actually know Him as their Shepherd. As we go through the first ten verses of John 10 we will do a check of our lives to determine who is our shepherd and see if we really let Jesus guide our lives. Let's listen in as Jesus is speaking to the religious leaders—the Pharisees.

> [1] "I tell you the truth, anyone who sneaks over the wall of a sheepfold, rather than going through the gate, must surely be a thief and a robber! [2] But the one who enters through the gate is the shepherd of the sheep. [3] The gatekeeper opens the gate for him, and the sheep recognize his voice and come to him. He calls his own sheep by name and leads them out. [4] After he has gathered his own flock, he walks ahead of them, and they follow him because they know his voice. [5] They won't follow a stranger; they will run from him because they don't know his voice."
>
> [6] Those who heard Jesus use this illustration didn't understand what he meant, [7] so he explained it to them: "I tell you the truth, I am the gate for the sheep." (John 10:1-7)

Back in the days when Jesus was in the city of Jerusalem, shepherds would bring their sheep near the city and gather them together into pens. These pens had high enough walls that predators could not get them. There would be only one entrance into and out of the pen. It was there that the gatekeeper would position himself. Nothing would be getting into the flock through the door unless that gatekeeper let it in.

Jesus is the only way—the only gate to go through—to become a part of God's eternal flock.[12] Anyone who promotes another way or many ways, according to Jesus, is a thief and a robber.

> According to Jesus, He and He alone is the only gate into God's flock and He wants to be the shepherd of the sheep. In this illustration, Jesus is wanting us to be in God's flock and to be our shepherd. Name some thieves and robbers in our world today that lead us away from Jesus to follow lies.
>
> _____
>
> _____
>
> _____
>
> _____

Once we have entered into a relationship with the Lord and have come into God's flock through our faith in Jesus, it is not automatic that we will follow Him as our Shepherd. To avoid this misstep in our lives we must make sure we hear His voice and not the voices of imposters.

> [8] "All who came before me were thieves and robbers. But the true sheep did not listen to them." (John 10:8)

In the flow of John 9 into John 10, and specifically what Jesus was saying here in John 10:8, we can see He was telling those Jewish people they were following the same people who cast the blind man out of the synagogue. Those religious leaders were the "thieves and robbers."

Unfortunately, many people follow the leadership of "thieves and robbers" only to be taken advantage of. How can we make sure we don't get led astray? How can we discern the voice of Jesus and know if we are actually following Him?

---

12   John 14:6; Acts 4:12; 1 Timothy 2:5-6

To begin to know if we are actually hearing Jesus and not a fake, phony, pretender, or "a thief or a robber," we have to turn around, look back, and retrace the trail of our lives and determine who or what we have been following.

Louie Giglio, a well-known speaker and pastor, has a great quote that clarifies how to determine who we are following. He writes, "You simply follow the trail of your time, your affection, your energy, your money, and your loyalty. At the end of that trail you'll find a throne; and whatever, or whomever, is on that throne is what's of highest value to you."[13] On that throne is who or what you and I are following. On that throne is our shepherd.

Reflecting on the quote from Louie Giglio and looking back on your life, what has been the highest value to you? What or who have you been following?

_____

_____

_____

_____

_____

To make sure we are following Jesus and not a thief or robber, we can also trace the trail of our affections. Whatever our hearts are preoccupied with will help us see who we are following. Jesus' affections were centered on one thing—the sheep! He committed His life to and for the sheep—for the people. The religious leaders among the Jews in that day were so focused on the Law and upholding the Sabbath that they forgot what being a religious leader was all about—to love and lead the people.

---

[13]   http://worship.com/category/louie-giglio-wired-for-worship-series/

If we are more interested in projects and principles than people, we are not following Jesus. If we do not love others well, we are not following Jesus. If we are preoccupied with ourselves (selfish) we are not following Jesus. It is good to look back and ask ourselves, "Where have my affections pushed me?" If it has not been about loving the sheep we have not been following Jesus or listening to His voice.

In retracing the trail of your affections, do you think you love people well? Do you think you love the people of God's eternal flock (i.e., Christians)? Talk about why you have this view of yourself.

_____

_____

_____

_____

Where or what have your affections, devotions, care, or love been focused on?

_____

_____

_____

_____

Another mark on the trail of our lives to see who or what we are following is the mark of our bondage. The marks we need to look for in our lives are those marked with what keeps us enslaved. Let me take us back a couple of chapters in the Gospel of John where Jesus was interacting with those who believed in Him.

^{31} Jesus said to the people who believed in him, "You are truly my disciples if you remain faithful to my teachings. ^{32} And you will know the truth, and the truth will set you free." (John 8:31-32)

A disciple is one who follows. If we follow Jesus and stay in His teachings (i.e., stay in the truth of the Bible) we will be set free from those things that keep us in bondage. Who or what are we a slave to? Worry, bitterness, dissatisfaction—not being thankful, staying distant from others? How about cigarettes, alcohol, pornography and things like these? We are called to be servants of Jesus. We can't serve two masters. If we are stuck in our sinful choices and are not bringing them before the Lord longing for Him to cleanse us from the unrighteousness in our lives, we are not following Jesus.

There are many things that want to pull us along in life like cravings, crises, causes, or cash. All of them offer a thrill, a challenge, and can get our adrenaline going, yet they can, and normally will, enslave us. If we choose to be pulled along by anything other than Jesus, we will end up being hurt and potentially hurting others. Let me be so bold to say, if Jesus is not our shepherd, *all other things* are thieves and robbers.

Does anything come to your mind that you may be a slave to that isn't Jesus? Share your story.

_____

_____

_____

_____

_____

We have the freedom to choose whatever or whomever we want to follow, but the truth is, Jesus is the *only* way to real freedom. Going back to John 10, notice what Jesus said about those who decide to be a part of His flock.

> ⁹ "Yes, I am the gate. Those who come in through me will be saved. They will come and go freely and will find good pastures." (John 10:9)

There are two results listed here that are guaranteed to anyone who enter God's eternal flock through Jesus. First, he or she "will be saved." Through Jesus alone we are saved for all of eternity. We are saved from being sheep without a Shepherd. We are saved from spending forever apart from the Lord. Later on in this passage we get these words from Jesus,

> ²⁷ "My sheep listen to my voice; I know them, and they follow me. ²⁸ I give them eternal life, and they will never perish. No one can snatch them away from me, ²⁹ for my Father has given them to me, and he is more powerful than anyone else. No one can snatch them from the Father's hand. ³⁰ The Father and I are one." (John 10:27-30)

I call this passage an explanation of the double grip of God. Once you and I are saved we are *always* saved. No one is able to snatch us out of the hands of Jesus and God the Father.[14] We will be with God forever. When that takes root in our hearts it lifts the weight of condemnation off our shoulders. It takes the shackles of performance off our wrists and ankles. It relieves us of the uncertainty that we may have done something that has caused the Lord to release His grip and let us go. The reality is, once we are in the double grip of God we cannot get out of it...ever. Nothing we do, or anyone else does to us, can snatch us out of His hands . . . nothing.

---

[14] see also, John 6:37-30 and Romans 8:38-39.

When you think about this total assurance of salvation, describe how that makes you feel toward Jesus?

_____

_____

_____

Isaiah 53:6 says in part, "All of us like sheep have gone astray, each of us has turned to his own way..." Given what John 10:27 has revealed, do you listen to Jesus, or are you going your own way? Explain.

_____

_____

_____

The second result we see back in John 10:9 for anyone who enters into God's flock through Jesus is that he or she "will come and go freely and will find good pastures." For sheep there is nothing better than that. To be a sheep and to meander around, chewing on lush green grass—that is true bliss. When Jesus said those words He was painting a picture of freedom and contentment. When we become Jesus' sheep and we follow Him as our Shepherd we will have the feeling of security, love, and care. Like content sheep in a lush pasture we will enjoy the life He is leading us to live. I'm not saying it will always be easy, but we will know true and lasting satisfaction. Many believe the lie, "If I give my life to Jesus it will be oppressive, confining, even enslaving." Actually, it is quite the opposite. Jesus is the only way to real freedom.

And, Jesus is the only way to real life. Jesus went on to say,

[10] "The thief's purpose is to steal and kill and destroy. My purpose is to give them a rich and satisfying life." (John 10:10)

This "life" is the theme of the gospel of John. It keeps coming up over and over again. We see it in John 1, 3, 4, 6, 8, 9, and now in 10 and it will continue to be seen throughout this gospel. Thirty-two times this "life" will show up in John's gospel. Jesus wants us to experience not just our physical life but a divine life. When we think of eternal life as a relationship with God there are two aspects to it. The most obvious is that it lasts forever. The second aspect of this life is that it is divine—or it has a divine quality about it. This quality of life is the theme John's gospel is trying to get across. It is a life with God—a life where we exist in Him—a life of following Him as our Shepherd. This eternal life is to know God the Father and His Son Whom He has sent (John 17:3). This eternal, divine life is a relationship with the Lord where He is our Shepherd and we are His sheep. This life starts today and lasts forever. This life is the experience God made us for.

Life with God, living in real freedom—this is what "a rich and satisfying life" is all about.

> Do you agree or disagree with this statement, "Jesus is the **only** way to three things—real freedom, real life, and real satisfaction"? Why or why not? Describe what "real freedom," "real life," and "real satisfaction" is.
>
> _____
>
> _____
>
> _____

Here is how I have come to know the abundant life Jesus is offering here: when we follow Jesus as our Shepherd and seek to live as He desires us to live, we will see Him actively working in our lives. Experiencing the abundant life—seeing God actively working in our life as we choose to obey and follow Him—is our Shepherd's will for our life today and for all eternity.

If we are not experiencing that sense of abundance, I don't think we are following the Shepherd. This does not mean life will be easy or we will be financially stable necessarily. I am talking about a heart of thanks and a sense of knowing just how blessed we are and how much our cup overflows. There is nothing better in this life than knowing Jesus is our Shepherd who touches our lives, grows us, and is our Rock.

> Do you experience the abundant life as Jesus would want you to, "seeing God actively working in your life as you choose to obey and follow Him as your Shepherd"? Share a bit of your story.
>
> _____
>
> _____
>
> _____

Chapter 6

"RECOMBOBULATION"

John 11:1-46

Traveling on an airplane is not as enjoyable as it used to be. With the constant threat of a terrorist attack, we have formed a search and seizure force called the Transportation Security Administration (or TSA for short). The agents, dressed in uniforms that resemble security guards, are constantly telling us to remove everything right down to the bare essentials of our shirts, pants, and socks. All that we bring on the airplane in our carry-on bags is inspected. Anything that goes beyond TSA's boundaries is confiscated. Then, we are asked to step into an upright electronic inspection chamber, lift our hands over our heads and get searched as if we were wearing nothing at all. We are then asked to step out, and may be picked at random to have a wand waved over our body or even a soft hand feeling for anything suspicious. Finally, we are free to get to our gate where we wait to board the aircraft, but before we do, we have to gather our things.

I was flying out of Milwaukee's Mitchell International Airport with my dad a while back and had just gone through the TSA routine. While putting my belt back on, my wallet back in my pocket, my cell phone in the other pocket, and collecting my things I looked up at a peculiar sign. It read, "Recombobulation Area." My dad went up to one of the agents to ask what that sign meant. I leaned in to hear the agent's response, "When you go through the line you get 'discombobulated.' Here, with all these benches to put your shoes back on and gather your things before heading to your gate, you can get yourself 'recombobulated.' You know—put back together."

At different times of life we can find ourselves feeling discombobulated. For instance, once a year, in the spring, for most of Americans we have to move our clocks ahead when Daylight Savings Time begins. I know that is not a big deal. Yet, for a few days afterwards we feel a bit groggy, slow to get going, a little out of sorts— discombobulated. The bigger ways we can feel discombobulated are quite obvious. Our lives can get rocked by events like a serious sickness, an accident, or a breakdown in a relationship.

When have you felt "discombobulated"? Share a story or two.

_____

_____

_____

_____

The Lord Jesus loves us so much He wants to guide our lives. When our lives feel like they have come apart in big or small ways, He is there to put them back together. When we feel discombobulated it is Jesus who can and will recombobulate us if we let Him. How that happens is laid out in John 11. Let's see what it says.

> [1]A man named Lazarus was sick. He lived in Bethany with his sisters, Mary and Martha. [2] This is the Mary who later poured the expensive perfume on the Lord's feet and wiped them with her hair. Her brother, Lazarus, was sick. [3] So the two sisters sent a message to Jesus telling him, "Lord, your dear friend is very sick." (John 11:1-3)

Mary, Martha, and Lazarus were siblings. They lived in the town of Bethany, just outside of Jerusalem to the east. Their world was discombobulated by this sudden and very serious illness of Lazarus. So, they sent word to their good friend, the One they knew could heal him. Jesus, at the time, was up in the Roman district of Perea, north of the Dead Sea on the eastern side of the Jordan River.[15] These sisters and their brother were torn apart emotionally by this sickness.

When we feel the struggles of life, it is often through them we can understand the ministry of Jesus in our lives most clearly. As we will read in John chapter 11 how Jesus worked in the lives of these three family members, I believe we will see four ways Jesus steps into our discombobulated lives and works to recombobulate them.

When I was a kid I used to play little league baseball. I was a catcher. When I knew my pitcher could throw a curveball, I would give him the sign to do it. That was the pitch that made many young batters nervous because when a curveball was thrown it looked like the ball was going to hit them. Then, at the last moment, it would curve and go right over the plate. It made the batter jerk out of his or her stance. It made batters feel insecure and totally caught them off guard. Sometimes life does that to us. It can make us feel insecure. Know this—nothing makes Jesus feel insecure. Nothing takes Jesus by surprise, or throws Him off. Even though Jesus was far away from the town of Bethany, He knew Lazarus was very sick.

When we feel our lives are on shaky ground or we feel insecure, what we will see first is Jesus wants to be our Rock.

> [4] But when Jesus heard about it he said, "Lazarus's sickness will not end in death. No, it happened for the glory of God so that the Son of God will receive glory from this." (John 11:4)

This sickness Lazarus had was awful, but Jesus knew all along why he was sick. He was sick "so that the Son of God may be glorified by it." When we get thrown a curveball, when life feels discombobulated,

---

[15] John 10:40

stand on the solid Rock of Jesus. It's not throwing Him off, and He just might use our circumstances to bring glory to Himself.

How do you "stand on the solid Rock of Jesus" when life feels discombobulated?

_____

_____

_____

Describe how our discombobulated circumstances have the potential to bring glory to Jesus.

_____

_____

_____

A second truth that we must hold on to is Jesus loves us no matter what we are going through. Our circumstances neither confirm nor deny the infinite love Jesus has for us. We just cannot always know what He is up to.

⁵ So although Jesus loved Martha, Mary, and Lazarus, (John 11:5)

Yes, Jesus loved those siblings and He knew Lazarus was very sick. So, look what He does:

⁶ he stayed where he was for the next two days. (John 11:6)

What? That goes so contrary to what we think He should do. If you love someone you run to their side! If you love someone you don't stall! In His perfect love, Jesus does the perfectly right thing. He knows the beginning from the end—we don't. His timing is exactly right—ours is not. No matter how discombobulated we feel, wondering where Jesus is in all of this, we know that His love for us never changes. Even if He may feel distant from us, He still is at work in our lives. His desire for us when life throws us a curveball is to strengthen our faith in the chaos.

Jump down to John 11:11. By this point Lazarus has died due to his illness. Let's see what Jesus told His disciples concerning the death of Lazarus.

> ¹¹ Then he said, "Our friend Lazarus has fallen asleep, but now I will go and wake him up."
>
> ¹² The disciples said, "Lord, if he is sleeping, he will soon get better!" ¹³ They thought Jesus meant Lazarus was simply sleeping, but Jesus meant Lazarus had died.
>
> ¹⁴ So he told them plainly, "Lazarus is dead. ¹⁵ And for your sakes, I'm glad I wasn't there, for now you will really believe. Come, let's go see him." (John 11:11-15)

Why did Lazarus die? Jesus said it was for the disciples' sake (John 11:15). This has happened so that they would "really believe," so their faith in Jesus would be strengthened through the mess.

In September 2013, cars were driving over the Leo Frigo Bridge on I-43 in Green Bay, Wisconsin, when they noticed a sharp dip in the road. Underneath the asphalt, the pilings which hold up the bridge and go deep into the ground were corroded. This weakened the foundation and caused chaos, but securing the pilings made the bridge strong again. Like pilings on a bridge, our faith is to go deep into the foundation of Jesus. When that connection with Him gets corroded, when we feel weakened, when life feels chaotic it needs to be secured and strengthened. If we let Him, it is Jesus who will bring life into order for us. Jesus will use our trials to strengthen our faith and make us more complete.¹⁶

---

¹⁶ James 1:2-4

How have you seen Jesus strengthen people's faith by having them go through hard times? Has your faith ever been strengthened when life seems to have corroded beneath you?

_____

_____

_____

_____

_____

Jesus wants to be our Rock, He loves us no matter what, and a third way Jesus wants to recombobulate our lives happens when sorrow dominates our hearts. When we feel extremely sad, Jesus is near and wants to comfort us with His presence.[17]

[17] When Jesus arrived at Bethany, he was told that Lazarus had already been in his grave for four days. [18] Bethany was only a few miles down the road from Jerusalem, [19] and many of the people had come to console Martha and Mary in their loss. [20] When Martha got word that Jesus was coming, she went to meet him. But Mary stayed in the house. [21] Martha said to Jesus, "Lord, if only you had been here, my brother would not have died. [22] But even now I know that God will give you whatever you ask." (John 11:17-22)

Everyone was very upset, confused, and broken-hearted when Jesus showed up. Martha knew if Jesus would have been there sooner He could have saved her brother and he would still be alive. Now that Jesus was there, she knew with His connection to God the Father

---

[17] Psalm 34:18; 145:18; 147:3; Isaiah 61:1.

everything would be okay. Then, Martha went to tell her sister, Mary. Let's go down in the text to verse 28.

> ²⁸ Then she returned to Mary. She called Mary aside from the mourners and told her, "The Teacher is here and wants to see you." ²⁹ So Mary immediately went to him. (John 11:28-29)

I picture Mary going quickly because she knew Jesus would console her. Oh, what comfort to know Jesus is near. He is near when your wife is dying. He is near when your husband has left you. Jesus is near when you just received a layoff notice. When we feel overcome with sorrow, know that Jesus is near and He enters into our pain. Jesus is not some distant deity that is detached to what we are going through. He is quite the contrary. When we are in the muck of life, Jesus gets down in the muck with us. He knows our pain and He feels it too and is here to bring us comfort.

> ³² When Mary arrived and saw Jesus, she fell at his feet and said, "Lord, if only you had been here, my brother would not have died."

> ³³ When Jesus saw her weeping and saw the other people wailing with her, a deep anger welled up within him, and he was deeply troubled. (John 11:32-33)

Jesus was intensely moved in His heart on how death is so hard on people, and with that emotion Jesus said,

> ³⁴ "Where have you put him?" he asked them.

> They told him, "Lord, come and see." ³⁵ Then Jesus wept. (John 11:34-35)

When you think of Jesus, I don't know what picture you paint in your mind of Him, but let this image sink in: Jesus wept. He cried. Mary and Martha were so distraught and Jesus felt deeply for them, just as He does for you and me.

Jesus was near and entered into the pain of those who were there when Lazarus died. Have you ever reached out to Him when you felt pain? How do you think we might see that the Lord is near when we feel sorrowful?

_____

_____

_____

Have you ever experienced the closeness of the Lord when you were really sad? Share your story.

_____

_____

_____

A fourth way Jesus wants to recombobulate our lives happens when we feel all hope is gone. Have you ever felt hopeless? Maybe you've been hunting for a new job and it just does not seem to be panning out. Or, you want to go to school but the timing never seems right. For some, your marriage is not what you thought you signed up for, and from your vantage point, it is not going to get any better. The list of things that destroy our optimism about our future can go on and on. So many people seem to have lost hope.

Martha, Mary, and everyone there felt hopeless. Listen to what some of them were saying,

> [36] The people who were standing nearby said, "See how much he loved him!" [37] But some said, "This man healed a blind man. Couldn't he have kept Lazarus from dying?" (John 11:36-37)

Can you hear it? There was doubt and hopelessness heard in the voices of some of them there. This is a truth to cling to—when all hope is gone Jesus wants to steer us to see the hope only He can provide.

> [38] Jesus was still angry as he arrived at the tomb, a cave with a stone rolled across its entrance. [39] "Roll the stone aside," Jesus told them.
>
> But Martha, the dead man's sister, protested, "Lord, he has been dead for four days. The smell will be terrible."
>
> [40] Jesus responded, "Didn't I tell you that you would see God's glory if you believe?" (John 11:38-40)

The order is very important: believe and you will see. Not, see and then you will believe. Martha, Mary, and the disciples all felt hopeless, but Jesus was going to do a great thing in that moment. They needed to just trust Him and He would show them His glory.

Trust is a part of life. Do you agree or disagree with this statement: "We have to trust in order to see the goodness in things or people"? Explain how a lack of trust causes us to *not* see this in others or in our world.

_____

_____

_____

"Didn't I tell you that you would see God's glory if you believe?" Reflect on how you may have seen the glory of God because you believed. Explain how a lack of trust, or belief, causes us to not see God's glory.

_____

_____

_____

In faith, we can come to the Lord through prayer, knowing that He hears us—He is listening.

> ⁴¹ So they rolled the stone aside. Then Jesus looked up to heaven and said, "Father, thank you for hearing me. ⁴² You always hear me, but I said it out loud for the sake of all these people standing here, so that they will believe you sent me." (John 11:41-42)

Earlier in the ministry of Jesus the disciples asked Him to teach them how to pray.[18] Here we can learn from His prayer. Notice what Jesus said here, "You always hear me." God the Father always hears us. He never shuts His ears to us. We know He listens because He cares for us.

Jesus wants to be our Rock when life feels so shaky—so discombobluated. He loves us no matter what and is near to comfort us with His presence. Jesus wants to be our hope and unbind the wrappings of hopelessness we can feel. He did this literally with Lazarus.

> ⁴³ Then Jesus shouted, "Lazarus, come out!" ⁴⁴ And the dead man came out, his hands and feet bound in graveclothes, his face wrapped in a headcloth. Jesus told them, "Unwrap him and let him go!" (John 11:43-44)

Just imagine being there! Jesus cried out, "Lazarus, come out!" Everyone waited. All the uncertainty, all the sorrow, all the hopelessness ... and then ... they saw him! Bound like a mummy, but he was alive! Then, Lazarus was released from His grave clothes.

What was dead was brought back to life. If Jesus has the power to bring Lazarus back to life, He has the power to recombobulate our lives when we feel so discombobulated. He has the strength to bring hope into our lives when in our hearts all hope is gone. He has the power to be our security when we feel so insecure.

Jump back to verse 23 when Jesus told Martha what He was going to do before He did it.

---

[18] Luke 11:1-13

²³ Jesus told her, "Your brother will rise again."

²⁴ "Yes," Martha said, "he will rise when everyone else rises, at the last day."

²⁵ Jesus told her, "I am the resurrection and the life. Anyone who believes in me will live, even after dying. ²⁶ Everyone who lives in me and believes in me will never ever die. Do you believe this, Martha?"

²⁷ "Yes, Lord," she told him. "I have always believed you are the Messiah, the Son of God, the one who has come into the world from God." (John 11:23-27)

Jesus asked a very pointed question, "Do you believe this?" Like Martha, do you and I truly believe Jesus is the resurrection and the life? Jesus being the resurrection means He rose from the dead, lives forevermore, and therefore He is the only way to have this eternal life. Do we believe He is the only way we can have any hope of an eternity with the Lord?

Life can be so hard at times. Our lives can be confusing. We can be bombarded with sorrow and uncertainty. Jesus can put us back together. He brings order and purpose to our lives. He reveals His glory. All we have to do is believe. Have we put our faith in Jesus to guide us? He loves you and me. Let's let Him recombobulate our lives.

The central point of this chapter is found in the very verses you just read (John 11:23-27). Why might those words be the most hope-filled words that have ever been recorded? Do you believe this? Why or why not?

_____

_____

_____

CHAPTER 7

OPEN TO LOVE

John 13:1-17

I can remember when our oldest daughter was going through her senior year and finishing up her high school experience. In the fall, my wife and I sat there at her last awards banquet for swimming. Then, in the spring we enjoyed her final soccer banquet. When the beginning of summer came we were there to see her graduation. This time was sweet and sentimental with so many good memories.

> Can you remember a time when you were coming to the end of something you really loved?
>
> _____
>
> _____
>
> _____

As we continue in the gospel of John, we now enter into the moments in the ministry years of Jesus when He had not months or weeks left, but His time with His followers would be measured in hours. The mood changed. No religious leaders would intrude for the moment. Instead, we have this warmth and tenderness of Jesus as He gathered His faithful followers for the last time before His death.

They had come to a large, furnished upper guest room above a man's house. It was Thursday night. As the twelve gathered, Jesus said to them, "I have been very eager to eat this Passover meal with you before my suffering begins."[19] He said this because he wanted them to know His incredible love for them.

> [1] Before the Passover celebration, Jesus knew that his hour had come to leave this world and return to his Father. He had loved his disciples during his ministry on earth, and now he loved them to the very end. (John 13:1)

Just like Jesus *loved* His own then, He *loves* us now at the same level. At the end of verse one, our translation says, "to the very end." That phrase can just as easily be understood, "to the uttermost," "completely," or "to the fullest measure." I like that it can be understood in these other ways, because it is true. Jesus loves you and me infinitely!

Take a few minutes and think about the last year. Has the Lord changed your thinking about His love for you (something that you didn't know or understand and now you do)? Explain.

_____

_____

How can we make sure we are in the process of understanding more and more what our relationship with Jesus is all about? What can we do?

_____

_____

---

[19] Luke 22:15

We can sing in our hearts an old song some of us remember singing as children, "*Yes, Jesus loves me. Yes, Jesus loves me. Yes, Jesus loves me. The Bible tells me so.*"[20] Jesus loves us to the fullest measure—utterly, totally, and completely; therefore, He does not want His love to be just words. He wants those who are His faithful followers, who have invested into their relationship with Him to *know* His great love for us!

> [2] It was time for supper, and the devil had already prompted Judas, son of Simon Iscariot, to betray Jesus. [3] Jesus knew that the Father had given him authority over everything and that he had come from God and would return to God. [4] So he got up from the table, took off his robe, wrapped a towel around his waist, [5] and poured water into a basin. Then he began to wash the disciples' feet, drying them with the towel he had around him. (John 13:2-5)

Here is the picture. They were reclining at a table that was low to the floor. Typically, people in Palestine in the first century would lay with their head toward the table, and their feet away from it. They would lean on their left elbow and reach in and get food with their right hand. While reclining, one of the servants from the house would go around and clean the dust and dirt off of their feet.

> It is important to know why Jesus was washing His disciples' feet. He was addressing an attitude His disciples had. They were arrogant and did not have a servant's heart. (You can read about it in Luke 22:24-27 if you'd like). How might we have this same attitude and how does it show up in our lives?
>
> _____
>
> _____

[20] Warner, Anna B. (v.1, 1860), McGuire, David R. (vv.2, 3), and Bradbury, William B. (refrain), 1862 (http://library.timelesstruths.org/music/Jesus_Loves_Me/)

What cues can we take from Jesus in this story so far to keep ourselves in check so that we do not develop the attitude the disciples had?

_____

_____

_____

_____

_____

As they were dining, Jesus got up and went to wash the disciples' feet. He did this unnoticed until He came to Peter.

⁶When Jesus came to Simon Peter, Peter said to him, "Lord, are you going to wash my feet?"

⁷ Jesus replied, "You don't understand now what I am doing, but someday you will."

⁸ "No," Peter protested, "you will never ever wash my feet!"

Jesus replied, "Unless I wash you, you won't belong to me."

⁹ Simon Peter exclaimed, "Then wash my hands and head as well, Lord, not just my feet!"

¹⁰ Jesus replied, "A person who has bathed all over does not need to wash, except for the feet, to be entirely clean. And you disciples are clean, but not all of you." ¹¹ For Jesus knew who would betray him. That is what he meant when he said, "Not all of you are clean." (John 13:6-11)

That really threw Peter off and it made him feel a bit uncomfortable. That's why Peter said to Jesus, "you will never ever wash my feet!" However, to truly receive love from Jesus we must allow ourselves to become vulnerable. Jesus answered him, "Unless I wash you, you won't belong to me." Jesus tells all of us, "I have to wash you." With that invitation, it is normal for us to feel awkward and uncomfortable, just like if someone told us today that they had to wash us. We tend to want to clean ourselves. To truly receive Jesus' love we cannot clean ourselves. We have to allow Him to clean us. That can make us feel exposed and therefore awkward or uncomfortable.

Like Peter, for many of us we have come to a point where we said, "Okay Lord, I am all in! If you want to wash me Lord, then wash not only my feet, but also my hands and my head (John 13:9). Here is my filthy, dirty, messed up life. Please cleanse me, forgive me, and take my dirt away." It is at that point we let Him love us, but I wonder if we let Jesus *continue* to love us?

What blocks us from allowing ourselves to be vulnerable to let Jesus wash us completely, to cleanse us from our sins and our guilt before God?

_____

_____

_____

_____

_____

When Jesus cleanses us from our sins it means we are forgiven and our guilt before God is removed. However, there is a daily cleansing that the Lord wants to do in us. He wants to love us by washing away the power of sin in our lives and cleansing us from things in our lives that are against His will.

A key point of the Christian life right now is to let Jesus wash our feet. For those disciples, their bodies were clean (they were forgiven), but, having been in contact with the world, their feet needed constant cleaning because the power of sin was still influencing them. We are in the world, and we are tempted, tested, tried, and are drawn away from the Lord by our own desires. Every day the Lord wants us to call upon Him to cleanse us, purify us, mold us, and change us. He wants us to stay vulnerable, open, and authentic.[21] He wants us to allow Him to love us today, for that is what a true relationship with Him is all about.

Unfortunately, many are unwilling to receive love from Jesus.

Why do you think this is?

_____

_____

_____

_____

_____

---

[10] Jesus replied, "A person who has bathed all over does not need to wash, except for the feet, to be entirely clean. And you disciples are clean, but not all of you." [11] For Jesus knew who would betray him. That is what he meant when he said, "Not all of you are clean." (John 13:10-11)

Jesus was referring to Judas, one of His disciples, when he said, "Not all of you are clean." (John 13:2). Judas had been with Jesus for years. He had heard the teachings, had seen the miracles, and even had his feet washed by Jesus there in the upper room. Sadly, Judas was shut off to the love Jesus wanted to give to him. The reality is, no

---

[21]   1 John 1:9

matter how much Jesus wants to love people, some will just not allow themselves to receive it.

Look what Jesus says next.

> [12] After washing their feet, he put on his robe again and sat down and asked, "Do you understand what I was doing? [13] You call me 'Teacher' and 'Lord,' and you are right, because that's what I am. [14] And since I, your Lord and Teacher, have washed your feet, you ought to wash each other's feet. [15] I have given you an example to follow. Do as I have done to you. [16] I tell you the truth, slaves are not greater than their master. Nor is the messenger more important than the one who sends the message." (John 13:12-16)

Jesus was teaching His disciples then, and us today, that He wants to work through us to bring this cleansing. Jesus calls us to bring His love to each other. And, according to the words of Jesus, to love each other is to be servants of each other in order to be used by Him to cleanse, purify, and get the dirt of the world and our own sin off of one another. Christians are called by Jesus to be involved in each other's lives in order to encourage, challenge, and guide each other. This is the calling and function of the church.[22] The purpose of this life as Christians is to love and serve people so they grow in their relationship with God the Father, Jesus His Son, and the Holy Spirit.

That sounds really good, but it is easier said than done. Some people are easier to love than others. We all come from different backgrounds and have our quirks and missteps in our lives.

Do you or I allow ourselves to be loved? Are we vulnerable enough to truly grow? Will we allow—even invite—Jesus to work through other people to cleanse us from our filth by giving them permission to speak into our lives so that we can grow in our relationship with the Lord? It's not easy giving and receiving the love of Jesus with each other.

---

[22] Matthew 28:19-20

What grade would you give yourself when it comes to allowing others to love you (A, B, C, D, F)? Explain.

_____

_____

_____

What grade would you give yourself when it comes to loving others enough to encourage, challenge and guide them toward the love of Jesus (A, B, C, D, F)? Explain.

_____

_____

_____

Is there ever a time when we should avoid loving others? Explain.

_____

_____

_____

If we love each other well, with the love that Christ puts in us, listen to the next verse.

[17] Now that you know these things, God will bless you for doing them." (John 13:17)

Jesus gave a promise in that last verse. In your own words describe what it means to be blessed?

_____

_____

_____

Have you known the blessings of the Lord in your life because you were involved in loving others for Jesus' sake? Take a moment and think about how Jesus has used you to bring His cleansing into someone's life.

_____

_____

_____

CHAPTER 8

I HAVE DECIDED TO FOLLOW JESUS

John 15:1-11

People are followers and who or what we follow is as diverse as we are. Some like to follow sports—whether a certain type or a certain team. Others like to follow the stock market. We follow the news. We follow people on social media. We follow our doctor's prescriptions, our teacher's instructions, and our parent's directions. We follow because it gives us something. We get entertainment, information, a challenge, or made to feel or be better.

For Christians, many of us want to follow Jesus. The Bible calls it being His disciples. A disciple is one who is devoted to learning and growing under the leadership of another. But, how can a Christian follow Jesus? Is it possible to follow Him when we can't see Him physically here right in front of us?

Throughout His ministry, Jesus called those who put their faith in Him as their Messiah, their Savior—the One who saved them from the penalty of their sins and gave them eternal life—to follow Him. We now come to what I think is *the passage* in John's gospel that gives us the clearest picture of what it means to follow Jesus.

In the last chapter we met Jesus and His disciples at the beginning of their time in the upper room as they were preparing to share the Passover meal together. Now the end of their time together was drawing near. Jesus told them, "Come, let's be going." (John 14:31b).

Leaving the upper room, they went out of Jerusalem and walked toward a place called the Garden of Gethsemane. On their way, there were vineyards on the slopes of the Kidron Valley leading up to the base of the Mount of Olives. I picture in my mind that it was a cool spring night and the moon shone brightly on the grapevines that the vinedressers were preparing for a new year of grape growing. Walking by the vineyards, Jesus stopped and turned to His followers.

> ¹ "I am the true grapevine, and my Father is the gardener." (John 15:1)

With the vineyards all around them, Jesus began with this truth—as a vinedresser or "gardener" takes care of a vineyard, the Father cares for us. If we follow Jesus, God the Father will help us. It always strikes me how our heavenly Father never leaves us to fend for ourselves. He is always with us, guiding, empowering, and helping us. One way He does this is by lifting us up in order for our lives to bear spiritual fruit for Him.

> ¹ "I am the true grapevine, and my Father is the gardener. ² He cuts off every branch of mine that doesn't produce fruit," (John 15:1-2a)

The phrase, "He cuts off" is not the best way to understand the original language here. The key to understanding these opening verses in chapter 15 is within the cultural context of Jesus' day. In the winter months the vine branches would be laid down on the ground to avoid being damaged by the cold weather. But in the spring, the vinedresser would gently raise that vine branch up off the cold earth so that it could bear fruit. That is the imagery Jesus was highlighting. So, instead of saying, "He cuts off every branch of mine that doesn't produce fruit," it would be more accurately translated,²³ "He *takes away* every branch of mine that doesn't produce fruit." He takes it

---

²³ As other English translations do, like the ESV, NKJV, or NASB.

away from the cold ground, or lifts it up from the earth. I imagine Jesus saw some of those branches on the ground, and knowing what was ahead—the hard times that were coming (His arrest and the fear that would grip the disciples)—He wanted His followers to know their loving heavenly Father would be there for them to lift them up when the times of uncertainty would come. Jesus wanted His disciples then, and us now, to know that God our Father wants to help us bear fruit even when times are hard.

If we are, figuratively speaking, laying down or feeling fruitless; if we are emotionally spent, physically exhausted, or disengaged spiritually, our Father in heaven desires to lift us up and take us away from that "cold ground" we are living on. He does this by giving us strength or encouragement in many different ways even in the midst of our difficulties. If we are heading into uncertain times and feeling lost and alone, we can call on the Father to pick us up. We know God wants us to bear fruit, so, we can ask the Lord to lift us up.

Have you experienced God the Father lifting you up when you have been feeling like you are living on the "cold ground"? How have you seen Him care for you like a vinedresser cares for the vine branches (if at all)?

_____

_____

_____

In a vineyard, fruitfulness is not just desired—it is a must! That is the whole point of the vineyard—to have bunches of grapes hanging from those vines. Pruning is a necessity in order to ensure that fruitfulness happens. Left to itself a vine will produce a good deal of unproductive growth. For maximum fruitfulness, extensive and skilled pruning is essential. Jesus carried that concept over to our lives lived in Him. In order for us to bear much fruit, God our Father prunes us.

² "He cuts off every branch of mine that doesn't produce fruit, and he prunes the branches that do bear fruit so they will produce even more." (John 15:2)

When my uncle passed away, my Aunt asked me if I wanted his chainsaw. We have a wood-burning fireplace in our house and I did not own a chainsaw, so I graciously accepted my Aunt's gift. One fall morning I wanted to trim back our lilac bushes, but the Internet said you should do it right after the blossoms fell. At that same time, I wanted to prune the crabapple tree in our front yard, but I read I had to wait until after the first hard frost.

People are similar to plants in this regard. We come in all different varieties. God our Father prunes each of us in unique ways. Sometimes He cuts away some of the excesses in our lives through inner convictions. At other times He does it through input from other people. And still at other times He will bring events into our lives that clearly grow us to be more fruitful for Him. The bottom line on how the Lord prunes us is by the use of His Word. Jesus had been pruning His disciples for over three years by teaching them, guiding them, and even reprimanding them.

³ "You have already been pruned and purified by the message I have given you." (John 15:3)

His message, His words—God's words—have been written down for us. It is the whole Bible that the Lord uses to prune us. In the book of Hebrews, the author was inspired by God to write these words,

¹² For the word of God is alive and powerful. It is sharper than the sharpest two-edged sword, cutting between soul and spirit, between joint and marrow. It exposes our innermost thoughts and desires. ¹³ Nothing in all creation is hidden from God. Everything is naked and exposed before his eyes, and he is the one to whom we are accountable. (Hebrews 4:12-13)

If we desire to follow Jesus, it is the Word of God that prunes us. It pierces our hearts and exposes our innermost thoughts and desires.

It cuts away at our wrong motives and trims our focus so that we bear the proper fruit in our heavenly Father's eyes.

> In what way has the Lord pruned you to bear more fruit (adjusted an attitude, made you more like a servant, helped you to forgive, grown you to understand His will for your life, etc.)? How has the Word of the Lord been used to prune you deep inside, exposing your "innermost thoughts and desires"?
>
> _____
>
> _____
>
> _____

Unlike grapevines, we can resist the Lord's pruning in our lives. We do not passively bear fruit. It takes a willingness on our part to invite the Lord's pruning. Following Jesus is something each of us must choose to do every day. With every decision and every thought, we must take them captive to the obedience of Christ[24] and decide to follow him.

I picture Jesus bending down, gently lifting up one of the grapevines with one hand and holding a branch in His other hand and saying these next words.

4 "Remain in me, and I will remain in you. For a branch cannot produce fruit if it is severed from the vine, and you cannot be fruitful unless you remain in me.

5 "Yes, I am the vine; you are the branches. Those who remain in me, and I in them, will produce much fruit. For apart from me you can do nothing." (John 15:4-5)

That is a bold statement, "apart from me you can do nothing."

---

[24] See 2 Corinthians 10:5

> In your own words describe what it means to remain in Christ (John 15:4-5)? What does it mean "apart from me you can do nothing" in this context ("nothing" in what sense)?
>
> _____
>
> _____
>
> _____

If we don't follow Jesus and stay connected to Him, we will dry up.

⁶ "Anyone who does not remain in me is thrown away like a useless branch and withers." (John 15:6a)

Inaction toward Jesus lets influences all around us suck the spiritual fruitfulness out of us. If we don't follow Jesus, we will be drawn to follow something or someone else because we are natural followers. The result will be a soul and a life that becomes like a withered dead branch, lifeless and fruitless. The result will be that our witness for Jesus will be wrecked. Look at John 15:6 in its entirety.

⁶ "Anyone who does not remain in me is thrown away like a useless branch and withers. Such branches are gathered into a pile to be burned." (John 15:6)

Who is gathering these branches who have withered in their spiritual life, putting them together in a pile and burning them? To figure it out we have to try and understand who they are as we look back throughout the context. In John 14:31 Jesus is talking about the people of the world. Then back to John 13:35 Jesus mentions all the people in this world who are watching us. Even after John 15:6, Jesus said in 15:18, "If the world hates you, remember that it hated me first." Taking these verses surrounding John 15:6 we get a clear picture that those who are burning the Christians who have withered are the people who are not followers of Jesus. In the context, if we choose to not follow Jesus our witness will be ruined. The world will say, "She's a phony. He's a hypocrite." Then they will lump us all together, cast a condemning judgment on us, and say, "They are all show; their spirituality is fake." Or, as Jesus put it, they [will] gather them "into a pile to be burned." The fire and the burning represent the judgment the world will place on us when we don't bear the spiritual fruit Jesus desires for us to produce. Vine branches have no use if they are not bearing fruit.

What influences or fears push us away from remaining in Jesus to bear fruit for Him?

_____

_____

_____

On the other hand, if we do follow Jesus we will see Him working in our lives. Jesus went on to talk about the positive affects of following Him.

> [7] "But if you remain in me and my words remain in you, you may ask for anything you want, and it will be granted!" (John 15:7)

"Ask for anything" we want and Jesus will do it for us? Anything? Jesus is talking about remaining in Him—following Him—being His disciple. If we want anything that He knows will help us bear fruit to follow Him well, it will be done for us! We will see Him actively working in our lives. Our lives will hang heavy with spiritual fruit, and God the Father will be glorified by our lives.

> [8] "When you produce much fruit, you are my true disciples. This brings great glory to my Father." (John 15:8)

Interesting, just because we are Christians does not mean we are disciples of Jesus. A Christian is saved. A Christian has entered into a relationship with the Lord by being born again (remember chapter one of this book) through putting their faith in Jesus to save them from the penalty of their sins. A disciple follows Jesus. A disciple invests in their relationship with the Lord. Not every Christian follows Jesus. We can see who are His disciples by the fruit that is produced in each other's lives.

All this talk about bearing fruit . . . what is it? We need to look around at the context surrounding these first eight verses in John 15 and see what Jesus was telling His disciples.

The first of three fruits we may bear will be the peace that only Jesus can give. Go back before Jesus and His disciples were in these vineyards to the upper room. In John 14:27, Jesus said, "I am leaving you with a gift—peace of mind and heart. And the peace I give is a gift the world cannot give. So don't be troubled or afraid." Another way to think about peace is the feeling of security even when our world causes us to feel insecure. The disciples were going to head into some very insecure times when Jesus would be arrested, but Jesus let them know that they would know the fruit of peace in the midst of the coming storm.

So, do you know the fruit of peace that Jesus gives? Explain.

_____

_____

_____

The second fruit we will bear when we stay connected to the Vine will be to know His abiding love.

⁹"I have loved you even as the Father has loved me. Remain in my love. ¹⁰When you obey my commandments, you remain in my love, just as I obey my Father's commandments and remain in his love." (John 15:9-10)

The world defines love in so many ways it can be hard to put a finger on it exactly; yet, we seem to know it when we see it. But what is the love of Jesus? The love of Jesus for us is His eternal, infinite compassion toward us. His love for us seeks no compensation. It is holy, pure, and uncomplicated. It flows from His very nature for He is love. All true love found in the universe comes from Him, for He is its source. Without abiding in Jesus we cannot know or be in tune with this fruit called His love. The only way to know the incredible heart of Jesus in an experiential way is to remain in Him, or to follow Him. Then, and only then, we will bear the fruit in our lives called "His love."

Do you know the fruit of knowing the love of Jesus for you? Explain.

_____

_____

_____

There is one more fruit that Jesus will bring into our lives as we stay connected to Him. We will experience His joy.

> [11] "I have told you these things so that you will be filled with my joy. Yes, your joy will overflow!" (John 15:11)

In the midst of all that was before them with the arrest of Jesus, His crucifixion, and the fear of being arrested themselves, what Jesus wanted them to have was the fruit of His joy, and He wants us to have it too.

Joy is a state of mind and heart that is not shaken by events that happen around us or to us. We may go through difficult times, or find we have to climb mountains of challenges in our lives. The Lord Jesus wants to be the running stream of joy in our lives no matter what we face. When we stay connected to Him, the cool water He supplies is that state of well-being and the calm delight that accompanies a close relationship with Him.

This chapter made a point that the fruit the Lord wants us to bear is *His* peace (John 14:27), *His* love (John 15:9-10), and *His* joy (John 15:11). How is that different from the peace, love, and joy we can get anywhere else? Would others say they see His peace, His love, and His joy in your life? Explain.

_____

_____

_____

The moral of this story in John 15:1-11 is make sure we are remaining in Jesus—staying attached to Him. We are going to naturally follow something or someone. It is best to follow Him. We must be in a place where God the Father, through His Word, continues to prune us. It is best to be around other branches that are attached to the Vine so we can bear fruit together. Ask those other branches if they can see His peace, love, and joy in your life. As we understand that we are by our very nature followers, each of us must ask ourselves this question, "Have I—truly—decided to follow Jesus?"

Have you decided to follow Jesus? Circle one:

Yes   No   Explain why you circled the one you did.

_____

_____

_____

CHAPTER 9

THE WORK OF
THE HOLY SPIRIT

John 16:5-15

At different times in life we seem to need different levels of help. At the start of life, infants need someone to help them all of the time. Small children need to be helped to get dressed, eat, walk across a street, or get buckled into their car seats. When our loved ones get older, it seems like they need help more and more. And when people get hurt or are not feeling well, they need an extra measure of tender loving care.

For most of us, we are so independent we don't like taking help from others. We may receive some assistance on a project or to get over some hurdle in life, but it seems like, more often than not, we take help only if we are forced to. For the most part, we say graciously, boldly, and with pride, "No thanks, I can do this on my own. I really don't need your help."

Have you ever had a time in your life when you needed help?
Are you one who finds it hard or easy to ask for help? How did
needing help make you feel? How about after you got help, how
did you feel?

_____

_____

_____

Now we come to the part of the gospel of John where Jesus is
about to leave His disciples. He wants to assure them they will have
all the help they need even in His absence. The question He posed to
them and us for today is, will we accept the help and utilize it?

We will start at John 16:5. Jesus is talking to His disciples.

> ⁵ "But now I am going away to the one who sent me, and not
> one of you is asking where I am going." (John 16:5)

Jesus starts with an observation, "not one of you is asking where I
am going." Actually, a careful reading of this whole interaction with
Jesus and his disciples shows that Peter did ask Jesus where he was
going. When all the disciples were with Him in the upper room, John
13:36 says, "Simon Peter asked, 'Lord, where are you going?'" Thomas
asked a similar question, "We have no idea where you are going, so
how can we know the way?" (John 14:5). However, from the time
Thomas asked that question until this time in John 16, Jesus was
teaching and no one was talking. Jesus was commenting on the long
silence and their mood.

> ⁶ "Instead, you grieve because of what I've told you." (John
> 16:6)

Jesus was referring to the intense words he shared in John 16:2,
² "For you will be expelled from the synagogues, and the time is
coming when those who kill you will think they are doing a holy

service for God." If Jesus said these words to you and me, I think we might be quiet and pensive as well. These are not the most comforting words. For the last three years Jesus had been with them and they had felt secure. Now they would be heading into times of great insecurity. A logical question Jesus knew they would be asking was, "Who is going to help us?"

> ⁷ "But in fact, it is best for you that I go away, because if I don't, the Advocate won't come. If I do go away, then I will send him to you." (John 16:7)

The "Advocate" with a capital "A." In other translations that title is translated "Helper." It was a name Jesus used for the Holy Spirit (John 14:16; 15:26). You may recall that back in the introduction I spelled out that God is one being, however, He exists in three persons: God the Father, God the Son, and God the Holy Spirit. In Christian circles this is referred to as the Trinity. The Holy Spirit is God. The title, "Advocate" or "Helper" is so appropriate, for no matter where we are at in life—because God so loves you and me—the Holy Spirit is here to help and support us for our best interest.

In this world there are only two kinds of people. There are believers and unbelievers, or saved and unsaved, or another way to say it is, there are Christians and there are those who are non-Christians. There are those who are born again (remember chapter one) and those who are not. No matter which camp you are in, God the Holy Spirit wants to help and support you.

First, Jesus addresses the help the Holy Spirit has to offer those who are unbelievers.

> ⁸ "And when he comes, he will convict the world of its sin, and of God's righteousness, and of the coming judgment." (John 16:8)

Notice the work of the Holy Spirit in the lives of those who do not believe is to convict. He will show that something is not right. He will stir in an unbeliever's heart a sense like something needs to be corrected. Jesus went on to break down three ways the Holy Spirit brings conviction into the heart of a non-Christian. First, the Holy Spirit will convict an unbeliever regarding sin.

⁹ "The world's sin is that it refuses to believe in me." (John 16:9)

The word "sin" is in the singular. The conviction is not for all acts of sin, but the Holy Spirit will stir in the heart of an unbeliever that simple singular sin of not putting their faith in Jesus. Our consciences may help us know that there are some things that we do that are wrong. However, in the heart of an unbeliever, the Holy Spirit will stir in their guilty hearts this need for a Savior—a need for someone to save them from the guilt they feel. The Helper, the Holy Spirit, will help them know they need Jesus to wipe that guilt away. When the Spirit works in a person who is not a Christian, the help He gives first is to convict them that they need Jesus.

¹⁰ "Righteousness is available because I go to the Father, and you will see me no more." (John 16:10)

Then, in an unbeliever's soul, the Holy Spirit stirs them to see the reason they need Jesus. The Advocate helps the non-Christian know they are not right before God the Father. He works in the heart of someone who has not put their faith in Jesus yet and brings the conviction that there is nothing they can do to make themselves right before Him. It is the Holy Spirit that draws each of us to realize only Jesus can fix this problem. Yes, God the Holy Spirit teaches us that Jesus is our righteousness. Only Jesus is perfect and holy. He made Himself to be the perfect and accepted sacrifice for our sins (more on this on the next page) and then He went back to be with God the Father. This leads us to the next verse.

¹¹ "Judgment will come because the ruler of this world has already been judged." (John 16:11)

"The ruler of this world" is Satan. Ever since the Garden of Eden²⁵ he has had a hold on humanity. It all started when he influenced Adam and Eve and they chose to sin against God—by going against

---

²⁵ Genesis 3

the Lord's rule and authority over their lives.[26] Ever since then, we have been under Satan's rule and the curse of sin.[27] The sin Satan induced has been judged at the cross. The devil has been condemned, and we have been freed from sin's penalty! The penalty of sin is separation from God. When Jesus died on the cross, He paid our penalty— He took our judgment. The Holy Spirit convicts an unbeliever that victory over the condemnation of our curse is found only in Jesus.[28]

The reality is the Holy Spirit convicts unbelievers of their need for Jesus to deal with their sin of unbelief (John 16:9), their lack of being right with God (John 16:10), and their need for Him to take the judgment against their sin upon Himself (John 16:11). Do you feel any of this need for Jesus today? Why or why not?

_____

_____

_____

The Holy Spirit helps believers too. The Bible, primarily in the New Testament, speaks of how the Holy Spirit leads, intercedes, gives gifts, helps Christians bear spiritual fruit, and binds Christians in unity and peace. Here, in John 16, Jesus speaks of the teaching ministry of the Holy Spirit. As He teaches us, He gives us what we need and only what we can handle, just like Jesus did with His disciples.

[12] "There is so much more I want to tell you, but you can't bear it now." (John 16:12)

Jesus gave His disciples what they needed. He didn't dump the whole load into their hearts and minds for they would not be able to

---

[26] Genesis 3:6

[27] Romans 5:12-14

[28] Galatians 3:13

bear it. Likewise, for the rest of our lives, the Holy Spirit will have more and more to reveal to us. As much as we need and can handle, the Holy Spirit guides us into the truth.

> [13] "When the Spirit of truth comes, he will guide you into all truth. He will not speak on his own but will tell you what he has heard." (John 16:13a)

"All truth" does not mean things we learn in our own natural way or ability like science or philosophy. "All truth" has to do with knowing the mind of Christ and what he reveals of His infinite truth. "All truth" is to know His will for our lives.

What hinders us from hearing the Holy Spirit? What hinders you?

_____

_____

_____

In my basement, I have a workbench that did not have any lights above it. When I worked at that bench I had a portable light I would turn on. Ever since we moved into our home, I've wanted to put some lights in the ceiling over that bench. I finally installed two recessed lights over my workbench. It wasn't as simple as I thought it would be. The trick was to figure out the wiring and tap into the power from the light switch. When it came time to connect all the wires I had to flip the 15-amp breaker in my basement off so I wouldn't get electrocuted. Out of curiosity I learned that about 220 volts comes into our house. That is down from where the power begins at the power plant. There, the power starts out at 275,000 to 400,000 volts. Then, by the time it gets to our houses, to give us just what we need, it goes through a series of transformers. That massive power got "transformed" to give me just the power I needed to turn on the lights over my workbench.

The Holy Spirit is like that transformer. He takes the infinite, massive truth of God and dispenses it just the way you and I need it. He gives us only what we can bear or can handle. To one person He shines the light of truth one way and to another He shines the truth a different way. He illuminates our hearts and minds exactly how we need it.

He also guides us in alignment with eternity. Jesus tells us at the end of John 16:13 this truth about the Holy Spirit,

"He will tell you about the future." (John 16:13b)

Some would argue Jesus was talking about what was to come in the immediate future for the disciples. Others say Jesus was speaking of what was to come in eternity. I lean in the eternal direction, because as we read the New Testament we see that all of this life is in preparation for our eternity with the Lord. It is the work of the Holy Spirit in our lives to help prepare us for our eternity.

There are two ways the Holy Spirit works in alignment with the way Jesus directs Him—in the context of John 16. He convicts an unbeliever to turn to Him (John 16:8) and He guides those who have put their faith in Him (John 16:13). Have you felt any conviction or any sense that He has guided you lately?

_____

_____

Take a moment to reflect on this question: What truth has the Holy Spirit brought from Jesus to you lately (e.g., how He has given you wisdom, a conviction about an attitude you've held, or correction with the truth about how He guides you, etc.)?

_____

_____

Ultimately, the work of the Holy Spirit in our lives is to bring glory to Jesus. Jesus made that clear in the next verse.

¹⁴ "He will bring me glory by telling you whatever he receives from me." (John 16:14)

> John 16:14 tells us ultimately what the teaching ministry of the Holy Spirit is all about. How can we keep ourselves glorifying Jesus in all things? How do you think that looks in our lives?
>
> _____
>
> _____
>
> _____

The Holy Spirit in our lives is not there for us to show how spiritual we are, or how powerful we are, or how in tune with Jesus we are. We do not have the Holy Spirit in us to glorify us. He is in us to glorify Jesus! He works in perfect harmony with Jesus and our heavenly Father.

¹⁵ "All that belongs to the Father is mine; this is why I said, 'The Spirit will tell you whatever he receives from me.'" (John 16:15)

The Holy Spirit reveals the truth to us. He wants us to know God's will for us. His help in a believer's life is to teach the truth about the heart and mind of Jesus. The Holy Spirit is sent to be in us when we place our faith in Jesus as our Savior.

When I was in college I worked for the Park and Recreation Department in Orange City, Iowa. A part of my job was to be a lifeguard at the local community pool. In order to be a lifeguard I had to get my lifeguard certification with the American Red Cross. One of the tests I needed to pass was to tread water holding a ten-pound brick above the water for what felt like forever (actually it was for 2 minutes). My feet were swishing back and forth as powerfully as I could move them. My hands gripped the brick like it was the most important object in the world. The water was splashing over my face, up my nose, and into my mouth. As I could barely keep from drowning, everyone was cheering, "You can do it! Come on Jeremy, just a few seconds more!"

In our lives, either in thinking how to get right with the Lord or how to live with Him, we are so independent that we try to tread the water on our own strength. As Christians we cheer each other on, "You can do it! Dig deep! Figure it out! Keep working harder!" The truth is, even when we try really hard, we often feel like we are drowning. Wouldn't it be nice if someone came along and gave us something to stand on—a solid foundation that would hold us up and lift the brick of our independence off of our hands? That's what the Holy Spirit is given to us for.

Is it too simple and easy to say we just have to quit trying to tread water all on our own strength and let the Holy Spirit lift us? Why or why not? How can we work with the Holy Spirit to allow Him to help us?

_____

_____

_____

If you haven't crossed the line of faith and become a Christian, has the Holy Spirit been convicting you about your sin of unbelief? The Holy Spirit has unveiled to you the truth that you need Jesus. Let Him help you cross the line of faith so you can enter into a relationship with God. Just receive that gift by faith, which means that you accept Jesus' death on your behalf and you trust in the eternal life He has given to you. When we place our faith in Jesus as our Savior (the One who rescues or saves us), He sends the Holy Spirit into our hearts and souls, and we become born again.

If you are a Christian, you know the Holy Spirit has desired to be your guide—to lead you into a deeper relationship with Jesus, to point your heart to eternity, and to make your life one that brings glory to Him. Let Him be your Advocate and Helper, let Him be your guide, let Him shine the truth into your life. Quit treading water on your own strength and on your independence and be dependent on Him. As a Christian, Jesus has given to you His Holy Spirit to be the solid foundation for you to know just how much the Lord loves you.

How do you feel you need to let the Holy Spirit work in your life right now?

_____

_____

_____

It is true, Jesus is not here physically, but it is to our advantage now that He has gone to be with the Father in heaven, because He has sent to us the Advocate, the Helper, or who is best known as the Holy Spirit. Let's let Him work in us today.

CHAPTER 10

LOVE AT ITS UTMOST

John 19:1-18

If you are a parent, you know what I'm talking about when I say my love for my children runs deep. Oh, how I want them to blossom and succeed. I want them to know my love for them, and most of all, I want them to know God our heavenly Father's love for them. His is a love beyond measure. My heart for my children is just a slight hint or reflection of the infinite love God our Father has for us.

On a scale between 1 and 10 (1 being very little and 10 being very much), how much did you feel loved growing up? Why do you give that number?

_____

_____

_____

God so loves us He gives, He guides, and He saves. When Jesus, God the Father's one and only Son (John 3:16), was born in that stable in Bethlehem and placed in the manger, He was sent here on a mission to rescue us. God the Father sent His Son to save you and me from being lost and alone, aimless, eternally purposeless, and separated from Him. There was only one way to snatch us out of the darkness and bring us into His marvelous light (1 Peter 2:9). There was only one way to restore our relationship with Him. The only path—the one mission God the Father had for His Son was, 'If we are going to rescue them from eternal death—eternal separation from Us—You, my Son, must die for them.'

As we read about the life and ministry of Jesus through John's gospel and come to John 19, the intensity level heats up. Jesus was agonizing over His impending death, and while praying he sweats drops of blood and said, "Father, if You are willing, remove this cup from Me; yet not my will, but Yours be done" (Luke 22:42). This mission was now front and center. With determination, He was going to take upon Himself the full punishment for our wrongs. The sins of us all would be laid on Him (Isaiah 53:6).

One of Jesus' disciples, Judas, betrayed Him by bringing the religious leaders to Jesus and pointing Him out to them so they could arrest Him. As they came to arrest Jesus, Peter (another of Jesus' disciples) took out a sword and cut the ear off of the servant of the high priest. When Jesus healed the man whose ear Peter cut off, He clarified that this arrest and ultimate death was what He was supposed to go through.

> [10] Then Simon Peter drew a sword and slashed off the right ear of Malchus, the high priest's slave. [11] But Jesus said to Peter, "Put your sword back into its sheath. Shall I not drink from the cup of suffering the Father has given me?" (John 18:10-11)

God the Father gave His Son an assignment—to suffer and die. Therefore, Jesus was arrested, led away, and tried by the high priest that year[29] who lead the religious elite with one goal—they wanted Him dead.

---

[29]   The High Priest's name was Caiaphas.

The death of Jesus is a historical fact. His death was motivated by God the Father's love for us. Jesus was determined to die to pay our penalty for our sins. Jesus laid down His life for you and there is no one who loves you more than He does (John 15:13). How does that stir your heart?

_____

_____

_____

Although this trial and impending death were to be performed at the hands of the Jewish leaders, Pontius Pilate, and the Roman soldiers, we must never forget that it was the will of God the Father who chose this cup for His Son to drink. The Father's love is so infinitely deep for us that it drove Him to send His son to die for you and me.

Let's unpack this Biblical passage in John 19.

¹ Then Pilate had Jesus flogged with a lead-tipped whip. (John 19:1)

When Pilate had Jesus scourged here it was to punish Him enough to satisfy the Jewish leaders without actually having to kill Jesus. Jesus would have been attached to a post and they would have whipped him on his back repeatedly. The scourging Jesus received was followed by being beaten and mocked.

¹ Then Pilate had Jesus flogged with a lead-tipped whip. ² The soldiers wove a crown of thorns and put it on his head, and they put a purple robe on him. ³ "Hail! King of the Jews!" they mocked, as they slapped him across the face.

⁴ Pilate went outside again and said to the people, "I am going to bring him out to you now, but understand clearly that I find him not guilty." ⁵ Then Jesus came out wearing the crown of

thorns and the purple robe. And Pilate said, "Look, here is the man!" (John 19:1-5)

Pilate was mocking both Jesus and the Jews, as if to say, 'Look at this pathetic creature' – "Look, here is the man!" What was so ironic was Jesus was indeed "the Man!" He was and is God, but became a man to deal with the sin that came into the world through the first man—Adam.[30-31]

Because we are born with a natural tendency to sin (our sin nature), we can't help it—we sin and fall short of God's perfect holiness. Why do you think people who want to be right with God think they can do it on their own—that they don't need a Savior?

_____

_____

_____

_____

The first man—Adam and his wife Eve—sinned at the very beginning of human history. Our sin nature has been passed down from one generation to the next ever since. In that moment, through the mocking, God the Father and God the Son were in perfect sync. Jesus knew He was doing what God the Father wanted Him to do (John 3:17), and he was fully committed to it (John 4:34; 6:38-39). I can't even begin to imagine how deep God our Father's love is for us that He would allow His Son to be mocked like that.

Along with the mocking, out of His love for us, God the Father allowed His Son to be scorned and despised by the very people He was sent to save.

---

[30] Of Adam and Eve. The name "Adam" means "man."

[31] Romans 5:12-21.

⁶ When they saw him, the leading priests and Temple guards began shouting, "Crucify him! Crucify him!"

"Take him yourselves and crucify him," Pilate said. "I find him not guilty."

⁷ The Jewish leaders replied, "By our law he ought to die because he called himself the Son of God." (John 19:6-7)

The law that the Jews were referring to says if someone makes themselves out to be equal with God, it is blasphemy or a great disrespect against God and punishable by death (Leviticus 24:16).

⁸ When Pilate heard this, he was more frightened than ever. (John 19:8).

Pilate was putting some pieces together and found himself thinking, "If this man is a god I cannot put Him to death." In the gospel of Matthew we see Pilate's wife gave her husband a warning, "Leave that innocent man alone. I suffered through a terrible nightmare about him last night." (Matthew 27:19). Yet, Pilate, filled with fear, tried to intimidate Jesus.

⁹ He took Jesus back into the headquarters again and asked him, "Where are you from?" But Jesus gave no answer. ¹⁰ "Why don't you talk to me?" Pilate demanded. "Don't you realize that I have the power to release you or crucify you?" (John 19:9-10)

Have you ever had anybody try to intimidate you? Have you ever been at the receiving end of someone's scorn? Share your story.

_____

_____

_____

If we have ever felt intimidated or scorned by anyone, what we felt is *not* what Jesus felt. He was not hurt or intimidated by the Jews or Pilate's words. He knew His mission—this cup that He was to drink—was the Father's will.

> [11] Then Jesus said, "You would have no power over me at all unless it were given to you from above. So the one who handed me over to you has the greater sin." (John 19:11)

I see two statements Jesus made here. First, this authority that Pilate thought he had was because God the Father had willed it—God gave that power to Pilate. Second, the one who delivered Jesus to Pilate was not Judas, but the Jewish high priest. Pilate was sinning, but the high priest had the greater sin. It was greater because the high priest knew about the Messiah coming and he not only rejected Him, but turned Him over to Pilate.

Let me share a quick story about my dad. But, I must start with his dad—my grandpa. My grandpa was pretty harsh with me. When he came to visit us he would see things around our small farm that he did not approve of. He would call me to come outside and he would point out to me how the barn needed to be cleaned, or the garage was in disarray. He would tell me how I was not being responsible and I had to get these things in order. I'll never forget the evening when my dad found out about how my grandpa kept reprimanding and giving me correction. My dad said to him, "You are not Jeremy's dad, I am. I'll correct him. It is not your job." The scornful look in my grandpa's eyes was now directed at my dad who took it for me. My accuser—my grandpa—could no longer make me feel guilty. That feeling I had of my earthly father's love for me is a small taste of the deep love God our Father and Jesus have for us. Jesus took the scorn, the ridicule, and the mocking for us and we no longer have to feel guilty.

Have you ever felt like you were scorned, despised, or rejected? Jeremy's dad took his grandpa's scorn for him. Have you ever experienced someone standing up for you, or taking a hit for you? How did that make you feel? Why?

_____

_____

_____

Before God the Father, Satan accuses us of our guilt, our shortfalls, and our not measuring up to God's perfect standards (Revelation 12:10). The enemies of God scorn us. But Jesus took the scorn for us. He stands up for us and in His crucifixion, He took the hit for us. What is your reaction to this truth?

_____

_____

_____

One more point about God the Father's love for us is that He loves us so much He allowed His Son to be hated for us. Jesus received sheer and utter hatred by the Romans and the Jews.

12 Then Pilate tried to release him, but the Jewish leaders shouted, "If you release this man, you are no 'friend of Caesar.' Anyone who declares himself a king is a rebel against Caesar."

13 When they said this, Pilate brought Jesus out to them again. Then Pilate sat down on the judgment seat on the platform that is called the Stone Pavement (in Hebrew, Gabbatha). 14 It was now about noon on the day of preparation for the Passover. And Pilate said to the people, "Look, here is your king!"

[15] "Away with him," they yelled. "Away with him! Crucify him!"

"What? Crucify your king?" Pilate asked.

"We have no king but Caesar," the leading priests shouted back. (John 19:12-15)

There was nothing Pilate could do. He was fighting against the Jews. He was fighting against his own conscience. Remember Pilate said earlier, "I find him not guilty." He was fighting against his fear. He was fighting against Jesus, who seemed determined to go to the cross. Ultimately, Pilate was fighting against God the Father, who out of His great love for us, was determined to have His Son die for you and for me.

Are you fighting against God? Could you be fighting against His love for you? God the Father calls us to respond to Him and His love for us by trusting Him. He wants us to trust in Him alone to make us right with Him through the all-sufficient death of His Son who died on the cross to pay the penalty for our sins. He wants us to have a relationship with Him. Describe your relationship with the Lord today. Are you fighting or trusting more?

_____

_____

_____

_____

---

[16] Then Pilate turned Jesus over to them to be crucified. So they took Jesus away. [17] Carrying the cross by himself, he went to the place called Place of the Skull (in Hebrew, Golgotha). [18] There they nailed him to the cross. Two others were crucified with him, one on either side, with Jesus between them. (John 19:16-18)

Listen to the words of the prophet Isaiah written about seven-hundred years before this event in Jesus' life,

⁴ Yet it was our weaknesses he carried;
it was our sorrows that weighed him down.
And we thought his troubles were a punishment from God,
a punishment for his own sins!
⁵ But he was pierced for our rebellion,
crushed for our sins.
He was beaten so we could be whole.
He was whipped so we could be healed.
⁶ All of us, like sheep, have strayed away.
We have left God's paths to follow our own.
Yet the Lord laid on him
the sins of us all. (Isaiah 53:4-6)

How does this chapter clarify for you the love that God the Father and God the Son have for you?

_____

_____

_____

_____

I have a hard time wrapping my mind and heart around how deep God our Father's love is for us. He loves us so much He caused our weaknesses, sorrows, sins, and rebellion to fall on His Son. He allowed Him to be mocked, scorned, and hated for you and me. Jesus suffered and died for you and me—willingly, "Shall I not drink from the cup of suffering the Father has given me?" When Jesus hung on the cross and died, love was at its utmost. When He breathed His last breath the mission was accomplished—His death paid our penalty for our sins. Because Jesus died, God the Father could now forgive us of our sins and declare that His justice against them was fulfilled in His Son's death. There is not a greater act of love in the entire universe than what God our Father demonstrated in that moment. He revealed His own love toward us, in that while we were yet sinners, Christ, His Son, died for us (Romans 5:8).

CHAPTER 11

GOD SO LOVES . . . NOW LOVE

John 20:19-31

For God so loved the world that He gave His one and only Son so all the people of the world could be saved from eternal damnation. God so loves us that He wants to have a relationship with us that can start today and can grow throughout eternity. He gives us abundant life, eternal life, living water to quench our thirsty souls. The Lord gives us Himself, the Bread of Life, to enjoy. He showers us with His grace. He transforms our lives if we let Him. He loves us so much He guides us along as a Shepherd leads His sheep—comforting, protecting, and bringing us to greener pastures. He shows us how much we need Him, for He said, "Apart from Me you can do nothing." He showed His ultimate love as He died for us. God so loves us—we've seen it over and over again in the pages of this book. And now we come to our final chapter out of the gospel of John, and here is what we finish with: God so loves us—now go love others.

> What are some things in your life that reveal to you that God really loves you in these three areas: (1) how He has given to you, (2) how He has guided you, and (3) what He has done to save you from the penalty of sin, hardships, and from the power of sin?
>
> _____
>
> _____
>
> _____

I love to soak in God's love, don't you? The truth is, God's love isn't poured out on us just so we can let it run over us. It is given so that we can share it. I think it is so incredible that in God's sovereignty—in His unalterable will and by His design of this incredible Gospel of John we've been in—we would end on this note. God's love is given to us, now give it away. We see this message clearly given by Jesus after He died on the cross and then three days later rose from the dead. This is how the final section in John's gospel begins:

> ¹⁹ That Sunday evening the disciples were meeting behind locked doors because they were afraid of the Jewish leaders. Suddenly, Jesus was standing there among them! "Peace be with you," he said. (John 20:19)

This was the very day Jesus rose from the grave. Mary Magdalene³² had just seen Jesus and came to the disciples as they were hiding and announced to them that she had seen the Lord. Then Jesus appeared to them and said, "Peace be with you." Jesus would say this two more times. When we live in the presence of Jesus we will know true and

---

³² Mary Magdalene was from Magdala in Galilee. Jesus met her in Galilee where he cast seven evil spirits out of her (Luke 8:2). She followed Jesus in his ministry. She was there at the cross when he died (John 19:25). She saw them bury Jesus (Mark 15:47). And she was the first to see the empty tomb and the risen Christ (John 20:1-2, 11-18).

lasting peace. When we know the peace of the Lord in our lives, if we are to love others, we must not keep it to ourselves.

> [20] As he spoke, he showed them the wounds in his hands and his side. They were filled with joy when they saw the Lord! [21] Again he said, "Peace be with you. As the Father has sent me, so I am sending you." (John 20:20-21)

Why did the Father send Jesus? Over and over again, we have learned, it was because of God the Father's deep love for us and His desire for us to have a relationship with Him that He sent His Son. Now, we have to join our hearts to His, and out of His deep unconditional love for us, we must love others. A way to understand what the Lord Jesus was saying is, 'As the Father loves you, I send you to love others.'

How do you think Christians are doing at going out with the love of God for others? How are you doing at reaching out? What holds Christians back from bringing the love of the heavenly Father to others?

_____

_____

_____

For most of us we may have good intentions, yet loving people with deep unconditional love is hard to do. We can receive God's love and be so grateful for it; however, loving others like God loves us can be difficult. I remember when I was back in seminary, Dr. Kem Oberholtzer, my New Testament professor, talked about how the Bible calls people sheep. Kem paused, looked at us and blurted out, "Sheep stink. And they bite. And they don't listen very well." It's true, we are called to bring God's love to those around us, but sheep bite, and they don't listen, and yes, some of them even stink. Left to ourselves, I think it is impossible to give God's love away. What Jesus did for His disciples, He does for us today. He empowers us to love others.

> 22 Then he breathed on them and said, "Receive the Holy Spirit." (John 20:22)

If we go all the way back to Genesis 2 when God formed man out of the dust of the ground, it says He breathed into his nostrils the breath of life. Then, when God set up a protective boundary for Adam and Eve not to eat the fruit from one specific tree called "the tree of the knowledge of good and evil," it came with a warning, "If you eat its fruit, you are sure to die." More specifically, "in the day you eat from it you will surely die" (Genesis 2:17). The day Adam and Eve disobeyed, sinned, and ate of the forbidden fruit, they did not die physically. However, what died that day was their spiritual connection to God. Their relationship was damaged and a separation from God ensued. This death of connection with the Lord was not only for them, but it has been passed down to all of mankind from then on.

The only way that connection could be healed was if a new breath would be blown on us. Jesus gives to us—breathes on us—the Holy Spirit. Now, with the Holy Spirit, we, like the disciples, can be in tune with the Lord again, united and connected with a new birth—being born again, born of the Spirit. With it we are empowered to love others.

> 23 "If you forgive anyone's sins, they are forgiven. If you do not forgive them, they are not forgiven." (John 20:23)

Here Jesus is telling us how to love others when they do wrong. Using the word "if" opens the door to our inability or lack of desire to love. We may not be able to forgive people when they have sinned. Ultimately God forgives and remembers sins. He is the Judge everyone will have to stand before one day. Yet, in the context of giving God's love away, we, by His Spirit, can be empowered and guided to love other by forgiving them when they sin or do wrong.

This calling to give God's love away must be governed by faith. To love others with honesty and integrity, being sensitive to the Holy Spirit's leading, takes a reliance upon the Lord in our lives. This is difficult because doubt can overpower faith.

²⁴ One of the twelve disciples, Thomas (nicknamed the Twin), was not with the others when Jesus came. ²⁵ They told him, "We have seen the Lord!"

But he replied, "I won't believe it unless I see the nail wounds in his hands, put my fingers into them, and place my hand into the wound in his side." (John 20:24-25)

Good old "Doubting Thomas." He just couldn't believe anyone could rise from the dead and live again.

Like Thomas, what doubts do you have about Jesus?

_____

_____

_____

When I was eighteen I ran the farthest I have ever run. My friend Todd, who grew up with me, agreed that he would ride his bike and carry the water as I ran from my home in Franklin, Wisconsin to the lakeshore of Lake Michigan just south of the city of Milwaukee and back again. All total it would be a thirty-mile run. I'll never forget it. It was going to be a hot summer day, so I started in the cool of the morning. Running to the lakeshore by the city wasn't too bad. I was in good physical shape and those first fifteen miles seemed pretty smooth. However, coming back—now that was a different story. The sun had risen high in the sky beating down through the hazy humidity. The rhythm of my feet pounding the hot asphalt was almost hypnotic. I could feel my energy pouring out of me as I pressed on. By about the twenty-five mile marker I was hurting. I didn't think I could keep going.

This idea of going into the world and giving God's love away can be exhausting and can cause us to doubt. Similar to when I hit that twenty-five mile mark, we can feel like we just can't do it. We know

God has set a course for our lives. We know we are supposed to bring His love to those we come in contact with. We know we are supposed to trust Him and lean on Him and follow Him—finishing the run He has for us. But, in our exhaustion we may start to hear that voice inside our head, "It's too hard." Doubt can overpower faith. So, what do we do? We call on Jesus. Jesus will lead us to believe if we let Him. Thomas wasn't left in his doubt.

> [26] Eight days later the disciples were together again, and this time Thomas was with them. The doors were locked; but suddenly, as before, Jesus was standing among them. "Peace be with you," he said. [27] Then he said to Thomas, "Put your finger here, and look at my hands. Put your hand into the wound in my side. Don't be faithless any longer. Believe!"

> [28] "My Lord and my God!" Thomas exclaimed. (John 20:26-28)

Jesus didn't leave Thomas to stay in his doubt. He led Him to believe.

Just when I thought I could not go on to finish that thirty-mile run, some clouds covered the hot sun and it started to rain! Oh, that felt so good. I was overpowered by this euphoric feeling. It felt like God gave me a gift. I had this extra burst of energy and the rain on my face carried me home to the finish. You sense that same feeling when doubt filled Thomas with discouragement and Jesus showed up, wiping his doubt away. All Thomas could do in his euphoria was to worship the Lord Jesus.

> [28] "My Lord and my God!" Thomas exclaimed. (John 20:28)

As Thomas was worshipping Jesus, Jesus seized the moment to encourage *us* to believe.

> [29] Then Jesus told him, "You believe because you have seen me. Blessed are those who believe without seeing me." (John 20:29)

To be blessed is to know the goodness of the Lord in our lives. We are blessed if we believe in the powerful work of the Lord. We can know joy deep in our souls if we believe that Jesus is alive and actively working even though we have not seen Him in the flesh. We are blessed when we can testify of His incredible love. When we struggle with doubt, we can call out to Jesus to help us. It reminds me of a man who lived back in the days of Jesus. This father brought his boy to the Lord in order for Jesus to heal him. His boy was convulsing from a demon who was in possession and control of the poor child. When the man asked if Jesus would heal his son, Jesus said, "Anything is possible if a person believes." I love the man's response. Believing Jesus can heal, yet struggling with doubt, he said to Jesus, "I do believe, but help me overcome my unbelief!" (Mark 9:24)

How could the man call on Jesus to help his son, and then struggle with faith? Can you relate?

_____

_____

_____

_____

We can believe in Jesus. We can believe that He died and rose from the grave three days later as our Savior. We can be Christians. Yet, trusting that He will empower us if we step out in faith to give His love away takes an extra measure of faith. We may struggle to really trust Jesus in the moment and we may doubt. Our fear of being rejected by our family or friends can shake our trust that Jesus is near and will care for us. Our fear of sounding like we don't know what we are talking about or coming across as incompetent may make us doubt if Jesus will use us to represent Him well. Our concern that we won't have the energy to love people the way the Lord wants us to can cause us to doubt if Jesus will carry us and give us what we need. So we echo to Jesus what that father said, "I do believe; help my unbelief."

What does it mean to give God's love away? Our mission is different from others who love other people well. The difference is in the message we give. We can love the poor by giving them food or shelter. We can bring justice to the oppressed. We can encourage the brokenhearted. All of these actions are ways to express love, yet anyone can do those things. Even though God is pleased when He sees us being kind and caring, what is different about bringing the love of the Lord Jesus to others for us is the message of love we are called to share.

Given what you have been pondering through this book, what would be the message you would share?

_____

_____

_____

_____

When we show and share the love of Jesus we need to talk about His love and His desire to have a relationship with them. When we love others we must encourage them to place their faith in Jesus to save them from their sins, for He is the only One, anointed by God the Father, who is the all sufficient Savior or "the Messiah."

[30] The disciples saw Jesus do many other miraculous signs in addition to the ones recorded in this book. [31] But these are written so that you may continue to believe that Jesus is the Messiah, (John 20:30-31a)

The Father sent the Son to rescue us from our separation from Him due to our sins, which again is our lack of holiness, our falling short of God's glory. Jesus paid it all. As an old hymn says, "My sin, not in part but the whole, is nailed to the cross, and I bear it no more, praise the Lord, praise the Lord, O my soul."[33] Those of us who have

---

[33] Spafford, Horatio G., "It Is Well With My Soul" Public Domain, 1873.

placed our faith in Jesus to save us are now declared righteous in God's eyes—we now have been made right and are no longer guilty of our sins before Him. Jesus came intent on His mission, and was passionate to accomplish it. We too must know our mission and be passionate to accomplish it. We are to go into the world and tell our family and friends, "Jesus died on the cross to save you from the penalty of your sins—which separates you from Him. And He rose from the grave to give you eternal life with Him. He came to mend the relationship that we can have with God."

This salvation—this relationship—lasts forever, yet Jesus saves us to give us a new life with Him today. He wants us to know His acts of mercy in our lives which are new every day. He wants us to experience His abundant presence every day. This life is available by believing in Jesus every day.

> [31] But these are written so that you may continue to believe that Jesus is the Messiah, the Son of God, and that by believing in him you will have life by the power of his name. (John 20:31)

Notice how John's gospel speaks of a belief that is a continuous action, "believing." We already discussed how Jesus saves us when we believe. However, the way we experience life—abundant life—the life and love Jesus wants us to experience—is by believing in the present tense, continuously, day in and day out, walking by faith, moment by moment. The offer of the gospel is a relationship with the Lord that starts today and lasts forever. Oh, that our lives would thrive in our relationship with Him, a relationship based on faith in Him. His desire for us is that we would overflow with His love as He sends us out into our world.

The Lord Jesus wants us to know He loves us. He shows us His love in practical ways. We will know His joy, His comfort, and His care as we walk with Him. Then, He calls us to give His love away. So, who are we going to love with God's love? Who are you and I going to share the Lord's message with, the message that God loves you and he came to earth to die for you and to give you life through a relationship with Him?

Was there anything you can remember from the whole book as you went through the gospel of John that God used to help you really understand His love for you in a more meaningful way? Was there anything that helped strengthen your walk with Him? Is there someone you would like to share this message with?

_____

_____

_____

Go and share this with someone.

GRACE THEOLOGY PRESS

Timely **Resources**.
Timeless **Grace**.

Birthed from a desire to provide engaging and relevant theological resources,
Grace Theology Press is the academic imprint of Grace School of Theology.
In a world where many say "truth is relative," Grace Theology Press holds fast to the
absolute truth of God's Word. We are passionate about engaging the next generation of
ministry leaders with books and resources that are grounded in the principles of free grace,
which offers a gift you cannot earn and a gift you can never lose.

gracetheology.org

CPSIA information can be obtained
at www.ICGtesting.com
Printed in the USA
LVOW04s0829071016
507568LV00006B/10/P